# THE YALTA CONFERENCE

# Problems in American Civilization

UNDER THE EDITORIAL DIRECTION OF

*George Rogers Taylor*

# THE YALTA CONFERENCE

EDITED WITH AN INTRODUCTION BY

## *Richard F. Fenno, Jr.*

*Problems in American Civilization*

READINGS SELECTED BY THE
DEPARTMENT OF AMERICAN STUDIES
AMHERST COLLEGE

D. C. HEATH AND COMPANY: Boston

*Offices*

| Boston | New York | Chicago | Dallas |
| Atlanta | San Francisco | London |

# INTRODUCTION

AS World War II drew to a close, a meeting was held in the Crimea which has become one of the most controversial events of the twentieth century. The caliber of its participants, the scope of the problems faced, and the circumstances of the time have combined to give the Yalta Conference a world-wide impact. In America, it has created an intensity of interest and a violence of debate matched by few subjects in the realm of foreign policy.

Yalta was the second, and the last, face-to-face meeting of Franklin Roosevelt, Joseph Stalin, and Winston Churchill. In their hands seemed to rest an extraordinary opportunity to shape the course of history. The spring of 1945 marked, furthermore, a time of transition with respect to the tasks and the relationships confronting America. The period brought the completion of plans for military victory and an increased attention to the political problems of postwar reconstruction. United States relations with Russia began to change from a partnership in arms to a state of cold war hostility. There ensued a protracted period of uncertainty. Indeed, one of the basic questions raised by the dispute over Yalta is this: At what point in this transition process were we in February, 1945? Should the United States have considered Russia an ally or an antagonist at Yalta?

This much seems certain. The negotiations represent the first substantial attempt to deal with postwar international relations, and as such they are a landmark in the emergence of the United States to a position of global leadership and responsibility. The worries and hopes and doubts of such a period, heightened by the personal drama of diplomacy conducted at the highest level, provide the stuff out of which controversies arise.

So Yalta has become a storm center of dispute. In considerable part the argument has been based on sincere and serious differences of opinion and judgment. But the intensity of disagreement has served at times to create partisan disputes rather than careful analysis and to substitute myth for reality. Part of the student's task is, as always, to disentangle one from the other. For some, Yalta has become the very symbol of failure in foreign policy; for others, it represents a necessary and commendable effort to reach agreement. The American representatives have been condemned as appeasers and praised as statesmen. Critics have traced many, if not all, of our subsequent difficulties in foreign relations to the decisions made at Yalta. But these same decisions have been defended by others as the best possible ones under the circumstances. Some believe that Russian aggrandizement was legitimized by these agreements; others hold that the basis for Soviet expansion is her violation of them. Still others are of the opinion that the decisions were without appreciable effect on later events.

The debate over Yalta has proceeded

on three distinct levels. The first of these involves the decision-making procedures of President Roosevelt. His influence can hardly be denied, but the critics of his decisions raise questions concerning the adequacy of his method of operation. Did he take enough advice? Did he take the right kind of advice? From whom did he take it? Did he try to run too much of a "one-man show" in his delicate dealings with Stalin and Churchill? On the other hand, given Roosevelt's own personality and ideas, what ultimate difference would it have made if he had employed different procedures? Closely allied to this question is the problem of responsibility. Can President Roosevelt be held equally responsible for all decisions made by the American representatives? Should he be required to act according to a prescribed procedure in arriving at decisions? Such questions as these can be meaningfully set within the larger context of the formulation and control of foreign policy in a democracy and the proper role of the President therein.

The largest part of the Yalta discussion centers on the substantive merits of the decisions themselves. Do the terms of the agreement represent, on balance, a success or a failure, a triumph or a tragedy, or perhaps the only realistic possibility for American diplomacy? If none of these, then how should the American performance be assessed?

In resolving this problem, the student must consider the conference both in terms of the setting in 1945 and in terms of the perspectives of the present. The critics of Yalta, although many of them spoke out at the time, have undoubtedly profited by their ability to talk about the happenings of 1945 in relation to a later course of events not known to the participants. Also, knowledge uncovered subsequent to the conference may reveal other possibilities of action which the critics feel could have led to different results. In all this, the careful student has the responsibility of recognizing when he is using one vantage point and when the other. He must beware of using hindsight as an easy substitute for foresight. When he says of the participants that "they should have known" or that "they should have done" something, he must be clear in his own mind whether or not this was possible given their knowledge and their circumstances. Finally, there remains for the responsible critic of Yalta the burden of placing himself in the position of the decision makers and presenting some realistically possible alternatives of thought and of action to those that were taken.

Whether one defends or criticizes the Yalta agreements, he cannot escape dealing with certain fundamental questions of fact and opinion. What were the objective circumstances of the time? What knowledge was available as a basis for action? Within what limiting framework of prior military and diplomatic decisions did the discussions proceed? What effect did these factors have on American attitudes toward the Russians? What were our objectives at the Conference, and what were our assumptions about the nature of Soviet intentions? Should these American attitudes, objectives and assumptions, or the ultimate decisions, or both, be criticized? Was the proper priority given to the various items on the agenda, and were the concessions which we made on the basis of this priority justifiable? These are the kinds of preliminary questions which will have to be answered before a final evaluation of the agreements can be made.

Beyond the realm of personalities and procedures, and transcending the circumstances and decisions of the time is a third level of analysis. The reader must test and evaluate different approaches to the nature of diplomacy and foreign policy. Should we judge the adequacy of the Yalta agreements according to standards of power politics or on the basis of certain moral principles? Or, if there is no sharp distinction between "realism" and "idealism," what kind of standard should be followed in conducting and criticizing foreign policy? What relative emphasis should be given, for instance, to total military victory, the postwar balance of power, the Atlantic Charter, and the United Nations in formulating a conception of "American national interest" in 1945? In the same vein, should we judge the results of diplomacy by a set of inflexible goals or should we expect the diplomats only to ratify the realities of power? What, in any case, are the limitations on decision making which operate on any diplomatic negotiation? A reasoned consideration of these questions will serve the student far beyond the confines of the Yalta controversy.

Part of the immediate background to Yalta and some sympathetic observations on the Conference itself are presented in two selections from Robert Sherwood's *Roosevelt and Hopkins*. This biography of Roosevelt's most intimate adviser has succeeded in recapturing the contemporary setting of the meeting, the cordial atmosphere within as well as the climate of opinion without.

From the shorthand notes taken by James F. Byrnes at some of the meetings of the Big Three can be obtained accurate accounts of what was said. Byrnes, a special adviser to the President at Yalta, records in these excerpts conversations involving France, German reparations, and the United Nations. His treatment, like that of all participants in the Conference, is a generally favorable one.

On the subject of Poland, the memoirs of Winston Churchill have been drawn upon for description and comment. The British Prime Minister was deeply concerned about the fate of that country, and frequently gave expression to ideas and objectives which were shared by the Americans. He presents a defense of the final settlement largely in terms of what he considers were the hard realities of the situation. For reference purposes, the complete text of the Yalta Protocol has also been included in the readings.

Two over-all criticisms of the agreements are presented by the British historian and economist G. F. Hudson and by the American author and journalist William Henry Chamberlin. Both men concentrate their attack on the Polish and the Far Eastern settlements, bringing different opinions and analyses to support generally similar conclusions. They question the wisdom of the American performance on all three of the levels discussed earlier. They do not approve of Roosevelt's ideas or his procedures; they criticize the agreements which were made and claim that, on the basis of existing information and conditions, they could and should have been avoided; finally, they object to the American approach to foreign policy, condemning it as unprincipled power politics.

Patrick J. Hurley, the American Ambassador to China at the time of Yalta, devoted most of his testimony at the "MacArthur Inquiry" to a criticism of those sections of the Yalta agreement relating to the Far East. It is Hurley's opinion that these decisions were immoral and cowardly, and that they played a major contributory role in the final victory of the Chinese Communists over Chiang Kai-shek.

A defense of the Far Eastern agreements was submitted at the same Senate hearings by W. Averell Harriman, who was present during those secret talks as our Ambassador to Russia. He stresses the military estimates on the basis of which we negotiated for early Russian entry into the war. He rejects Hurley's views that Yalta had an adverse effect on China, and emphasizes, instead, Soviet violation of her agreements and treaties.

In the eyes of Chester Wilmot, Yalta was "Stalin's Greatest Victory." This British historian brings fresh perspectives to support his contention. He stresses, for example, the impact of the military situation on the Conference and the problems of Anglo-American relationships. His main thesis is that the nonpolitical American approach to war caused us to disregard the power factors in international relations, and that this blindspot cost us insight, if not success, in planning for the postwar world at Yalta. Wilmot's opinion presents an interesting contrast with those other criticisms which take the Americans to task for playing cynical power politics.

A semiofficial balance sheet of the Crimean Conference as a successful attempt to establish the possibilities of peace has been drawn up by the American Secretary of State in 1945, Edward Stettinius. He defends Yalta on each level of controversy, the personalities, the decisions, and the framework within which we operated.

The final selection is a series of excerpts from the Senate hearings on Charles E. Bohlen's nomination as Ambassador to Russia in 1953. As interpreter and adviser, he was at the side of the President in all his negotiations with Stalin. It is Bohlen's position that, on balance, the decisions were the best possible ones and that they have had little or no effect on later developments. Of the Senators who interrogated Bohlen, Homer Ferguson (R. Mich.), William Knowland (R. Cal.), Bourke Hickenlooper (R. Iowa), and H. Alexander Smith (R. N. J.) all have vigorously condemned the wartime conference. Taken together, these questions and answers provide a partial summing up and balancing of issues which continue to trouble and divide Americans.

For thoughtful people, the many debates, great and small, on American foreign policy have been opportunities for self-examination as well as for controversy. This case study invites the reader to engage in both. Americans did not solicit the role and the responsibilities of a world leader. Indeed, by tradition and by temperament, we may not be particularly well qualified to assume such a position. Yet it is inescapable. As the Yalta Conference demonstrates, we are deeply and deliberately involved in world affairs. Our government is confronted daily with the complexities of decision making in matters of international importance. For the citizen, there is the parallel obligation to think critically and constructively about our position in the world.

[Note: The statement in the "Clash of Issues" on page xi by Arthur Bliss Lane is quoted from I Saw Poland Betrayed (New York, 1948), pp. 84, 306; that by Henry Steele Commager from "Was Yalta a Calamity? A Debate," New York Times Magazine, August 3, 1952, p. 49. Both statements reprinted with permission.]

# CONTENTS

# THE CLASH OF ISSUES

### Was the conference a success?

The second conference of the Big Three held at Yalta in February 1945 represented the high point of Soviet diplomatic success and correspondingly the low point of American appeasement.

WILLIAM HENRY CHAMBERLIN

The record of the conference shows clearly that the Soviet Union made greater concessions at Yalta to the United States and Great Britain than were made to the Soviets. The agreements reached among President Roosevelt, Prime Minister Churchill and Marshal Stalin were, on the whole, a diplomatic triumph for the United States and Great Britain.     EDWARD R. STETTINIUS, JR.

### What of the Polish agreement?

The Yalta agreement with respect to Poland was . . . a capitulation on the part of the United States and Great Britain to the views of the Soviet Union. . . . (It) was the deathblow to Poland's hopes for independence and for a democratic form of government.

ARTHUR BLISS LANE

I don't consider that the agreement at Yalta involved a surrender. It involved the opposite. . . . The fact that they violated it I don't think means that the agreement was bad. . . . I have never been able to see afterward that you could have done much more that would have been of benefit to Poland or the Polish people.

CHARLES E. BOHLEN

### What of the Far Eastern Settlement?

American diplomats surrendered the territorial integrity and the political independence of China, surrendered the principles of the Atlantic Charter, and wrote the blueprint for the Communist conquest of China in secret agreement at Yalta.

PATRICK J. HURLEY

Nothing that was done at Yalta contributed to the loss of control over China by Chiang Kai-shek. The Yalta understanding was implemented by the Sino-Soviet agreements, which had they been carried out by Stalin might have saved the Chinese National Government.     W. AVERELL HARRIMAN

### What is the best approach to the problems involved?

The real issue for the world and for the future is not what Stalin would or could have taken, but what he was given the right to take. This agreement provided Stalin with a moral cloak for his aggressive designs . . .     CHESTER WILMOT

Aside from such things as the restoration of Russian sovereignty in Sakhalin and the Kuriles, the Western allies conceded nothing that Russia did not already have or could not have taken.

HENRY STEELE COMMAGER

# Harry L. Hopkins: THE GENESIS OF THE YALTA CONFERENCE

AS early as the middle of September, 1944, the President was contemplating a second conference with Stalin and Churchill. There were a variety of pressing problems which the President believed warranted such a conference and both Churchill and Stalin were agreeable to the conference. Churchill was, indeed, insistent on it. The reasons were obvious.

By this time we had agreed upon our full-out and final assault on the German citadel and yet there were no firm agreements as to what was to be done with Germany once she was defeated. The machinery of the European Advisory Council moved so slowly that it was quite possible to visualize the collapse of Germany without any plans or agreements having been made.

Although at Teheran Stalin had made a firm commitment in so far as Soviet participation in the war against Japan was concerned, that needed to be clarified as to precise dates and the extent of Soviet participation.

On the political side there was no agreement as to reparations against Germany; the problem of dismemberment of the Reich was hanging fire; there was no agreement as to zones; nothing as to whether or not we were going to encourage or discourage a central German Government or, indeed, in what way the Allies were going to utilize German machinery. The policy toward war criminals was stalemated; the earmarks of trouble in Poland were already obvious — neither the eastern frontier nor the western frontier was settled. Our whole policy toward the Far East needed a thorough-going understanding, particularly so far as the Soviet Union was concerned. We knew from Teheran that the Russians wanted certain things as a condition to their declaring war on Japan or, at any rate, they said they wanted them and it was extremely important for the United States in particular, in view of our historic relationship with China, to protect China's interests in these negotiations. Things regarding the Far East had to be settled otherwise we might find the three allies going their separate ways. The place of France in European and world affairs was in an irritating state. France wanted a Zone of Occupation. She had not been given one. France wanted to be on any Control Commission governing Germany. The Allies had given her no assurances on this point. France wanted a clear-cut statement regarding the Allies' ambitions in the French Empire, particularly Indo-China. France had good reason to believe that President Roosevelt was not enthusiastic about returning Indo-China to the Empire, and was thoroughly suspicious of the Allies on this point. France wanted to have a full part in world affairs and the decision on this point, if not made at an early date, would cause endless troubles. Furthermore, there was the hang-over of the Dumbarton Oaks United Nations Conference. The voting procedure had not been settled. There seemed to be no way to settle it except by the three heads of state getting together. Indeed, all of the things I have mentioned would, in my opinion, have been hopelessly delayed without a conference.

The President, as usual, began to play with ideas about places for the conference and suggested a wide variety of locations, none of which included Russia. I told the President, as soon as the discussion started, that there was not a chance of getting Stalin out of Russia at this time in the light of the military situation on Germany's eastern front and that if he did not look out we would wind up with a lot of long-winded, irritating cables back and forth getting exactly nowhere and that we might as well make up our minds first at least to go to some convenient point in Russia — preferably in the Crimea. The President was not opposed to this but in view of the forthcoming elections, considered it to be unwise. About this time, too, it became perfectly clear that the President had to conduct a vigorous campaign for the election, which made a conference prior to election out of the question. And, because he felt it to his political disadvantage to indicate Russia as the place of the meeting, he postponed all discussion of the place until after the election was over. As soon as the election had taken place I saw Gromyko, the Russian Ambassador, and told him that we wanted to arrange the conference. Gromyko said that he knew Stalin was prepared for the conference but that he doubted that he could leave Russia in view of the great Soviet offensive against Germany. I asked Gromyko whether there was any place in the Crimea at which it was fit to hold a conference, and he said he was sure there was but made no further comment. A couple of weeks later the President got a message from Stalin saying he understood the President was willing to go to the Crimea and suggesting Yalta as a desirable place. This was the first indication anyone around the President had that the President would even consider a conference in Russia. All of the President's close advisers were opposed to his going to Russia; most did not like or trust the Russians anyway and could not understand why the President of the United States should cart himself all over the world to meet Stalin. This argument carried no weight with me. The all-important thing was to get the meeting. There was not a chance of getting that meeting outside of the Crimea. The President's advisers gave me a lot of acid criticism when they found out that I was the one who had talked to Gromyko about the possibility of going to the Crimea. When they descended on the President to urge him not to go the President wavered again and cooked up a lot of counter proposals, none of which made any sense. I was sure the President would wind up by going to the Crimea, the primary reason being that it was a part of the world he had never visited and his adventurous spirit was forever leading him to go to unusual places and, on his part, the election being over, he would no longer be disturbed about it for political reasons.

Churchill was none too keen about the Crimea because he prefers a warm climate and more comfort than he thought the Crimea could afford, but he was so anxious to have the meeting that he would have gone to Moscow if necessary.

The holidays were then coming on, the President had to open the Congressional session and negotiations were then entered into and naval officers and embassy officials in Moscow hurried to the Crimea to find out if the physical conditions were such as to warrant the President going to Yalta. Harriman's report was in the affirmative.

# *James F. Byrnes*: YALTA—HIGH TIDE OF BIG THREE UNITY

WE were at sea on the President's birthday, January 30, and his daughter, Mrs. John Boettiger, made the birthday dinner a gala occasion. Gifts purchased from the ship's commissary were presented to the President. His devoted Filipino chef insisted on providing a birthday cake. But others had the same idea. The commissioned officers presented one; so did the enlisted men and the warrant officers. When four cakes arrived, one of our group, who remembered that the President had just been inaugurated to serve a fourth term, went out and procured a fifth cake. A large candle was stuck into it which the President was challenged to blow out.

Although he responded to the gaiety of the occasion, I was disturbed by his appearance. I feared his illness was not due entirely to a cold and expressed this concern to Mrs. Boettiger. She thought my opinion arose from observing him during the moving pictures, when she usually sat on one side of the President and I on the other. She explained that, while looking at the pictures, the President would have his mouth open because of his sinus trouble and that this made him look badly, but he was not really ill. Dr. McIntyre also expressed the belief that the President's appearance was due to the combination of sinus infection and cold. Since he had so often "bounced back" after an illness, I dismissed my fears.

By the time we reached Malta he had improved greatly. As the *Quincy* approached its anchorage we saw Prime Minister Churchill, in navy uniform, waving a greeting to the President from the deck of the H.M.S. *Sirius* across the channel. Shortly thereafter he and his daughter, Section Officer Sarah Oliver, came aboard for lunch. There were ten of us at lunch and discussion of the approaching conference was only general. The President did, however, confide to Churchill his plans to visit King Ibn Saud on his return trip to discuss the Palestine question. He wanted to bring about peace between the Arabs and the Jews. Churchill wished him good luck but didn't seem very hopeful that the President would meet with success. He didn't.

That night the President traveled for the first time in the Sacred Cow. Months earlier I had tried to induce him to use this airplane, built for his use and provided with an elevator which could be lowered from the plane to the ground, for his trips to Hyde Park and Warm Springs. He told me he disliked to fly; he disliked the monotony of looking at the clouds. His other objection was more surprising. He thought an unnecessary expense had been incurred in fitting a plane solely for his personal use. He said he had not been consulted about it and he did not approve it. This from a man who often had been accused of being the greatest spender ever to hold the office of President!

So far as I could see, the President had

made little preparation for the Yalta Conference. His inauguration had taken place the Saturday before we left and for ten days preceding that he had been overwhelmed with engagements. On the cruiser, the President, Admiral Leahy and I, on four or five occasions, usually after dinner, discussed some of the questions to be considered, particularly the proposal for the United Nations. But not until the day before we landed at Malta did I learn that we had on board a very complete file of studies and recommendations prepared by the State Department. I asked the President if the Department had given him any material and he advised me it was all in the custody of Lieutenant William M. Rigdon. Later, when I saw some of these splendid studies I greatly regretted they had not been considered on board ship. I am sure the failure to study them while en route was due to the President's illness. And I am sure that only President Roosevelt, with his intimate knowledge of the problems, could have handled the situation so well with so little preparation.

Secretary of State Edward R. Stettinius, who had gone ahead by air, joined us at Malta. We were met also by Mr. Hopkins who had been visiting in London, Paris and Rome. Harry was sick. He took off for Yalta in the first available airplane and during the conference was confined to his bed most of the time. His great courage caused him to attend every session of the conference, but immediately after adjournment he would retire to his room. Members of our delegation frequently held meetings there because Dr. McIntyre insisted he remain in bed.

There were some uneasy minds in our party as we took off from Malta. Our pilots were unfamiliar with the airfield at Saki where, we understood, there had

been a considerable snowfall. We had conflicting reports on the hazards of the drive from Saki across the mountains to Yalta. There also was some fear of typhus, as we were told the Germans had left the place infested with vermin.

These worries were based on an underestimation of the prodigious effort the Russians exerted to demonstrate their hospitality. The landing strip at Saki was swept clear of every snowflake. The road from the field to Yalta, eighty miles away, was guarded by an unbroken line of Soviet troops, many of them girls — girls with guns. Livadia Palace, which was our headquarters and the scene of the meetings, was immaculate. We were told the Germans had completely ransacked it, leaving behind only two paintings out of all the furnishings in the huge building which had been a summer home for the Czars. Although some of the conveniences we fortunate Americans are accustomed to were missing, the Russians, with only three weeks advance notice, had done an amazing job in completely renovating the place.

As we were shown to our rooms we were told what they had been used for when the Czars were in residence. We soon learned Fleet Admiral Ernest J. King had been assigned to the Czarina's boudoir. He was reminded of it throughout the conference.

The Yalta Conference opened on Sunday, February 4, 1945, on a rising tide of Allied victories. The German counteroffensive in the west had been stopped in the bloody snow of the Ardennes Forest, and we were preparing to launch our drive across the Rhine. The Russians had begun the drive on Germany's eastern frontier that was to end in Berlin three months later. The situation was such that at one time President Roosevelt and Marshal Stalin engaged in light banter as to whether they should wager that the Red Army would get to Berlin before the American Army recaptured Manila.

Our chief objective for the conference was to secure agreement on the Dumbarton Oaks proposal for the creation of an international peace organization. But the rapid advance of our armies required also that urgent consideration be given to European political and military problems. It was natural, then, that the President, with the agreement of the other members, opened the conference with the suggestion to discuss "what we shall do with Germany."

Stalin immediately made it clear that he wanted to discuss the terms of the German surrender, the future form of the German state or states, reparations, and the allocation of a zone of occupation to France.

In the fall of 1944 the Soviet Union and the Provisional Government of France had entered into a treaty of friendship. It was immediately obvious at Yalta, however, that the treaty and the friendly words exchanged over it by the diplomats had not changed in any degree Marshal Stalin's opinion on the contribution of France to the war. He thought France should play little part in the control of Germany, and stated that Yugoslavia and Poland were more entitled to consideration than France.

When Roosevelt and Churchill proposed that France be allotted a zone of occupation, Stalin agreed. But it was clear he agreed only because the French zone was to be taken out of the territory allotted to the United States and the United Kingdom. And he especially opposed giving France a representative on the Allied Control Council for Germany. He undoubtedly concurred in the opinion

expressed to the President by Mr. Molotov that this should be done "only as a kindness to France and not because she is entitled to it."

"I am in favor of France being given a zone," Stalin declared, "but I cannot forget that in this war France opened the gates to the enemy." He maintained it would create difficulties to give France a zone of occupation and a representative on the Allied Control Council and refuse the same treatment to others who had fought more than France. He said France would soon demand that de Gaulle attend the Big Three's conferences.

Churchill argued strongly in favor of France's being represented on the Council. He said the British public would not understand if questions affecting France and the French zone were settled without her participation in the discussion. It did not follow, as Stalin had suggested, that France would demand de Gaulle's participation in the conferences of the Big Three, he added. And, in his best humor, Mr. Churchill said the conference was "a very exclusive club, the entrance fee being at least five million soldiers or the equivalent."

Stalin, however, feared there would be such a demand. He said General de Gaulle was "very unrealistic," and reiterated that even though "France had not done much fighting in the war, yet de Gaulle has demanded equal rights with the Soviets, the British and the Americans, who have done the fighting."

President Roosevelt did not take issue with Stalin on de Gaulle. The President had great admiration for France and its people but he did not admire de Gaulle. On several occasions he referred to a conversation at Casablanca in which de Gaulle compared himself with Joan of Arc as the spiritual leader of France, and with Clemenceau as the political leader.

President Roosevelt's first opinion was not to insist upon giving France representation on the Allied Council if she were allotted a zone. As the argument proceeded, however, the President said he wished to consider further that phase of the question and asked that action be delayed. The following day Mr. Hopkins, Averell Harriman, our Ambassador to the Soviet Union, and I urged upon the President the view that France should be represented on the Council, that they could not accept a zone without such representation, and that any other action would greatly humiliate them. The President finally reached the same conclusion, and he later succeeded in inducing Stalin to agree with him.

The major problem in connection with the surrender of Germany arose from an informal suggestion, broached at Teheran, that the future security of Europe required Germany to be cut up into a number of individual states.

The discussion was brief but there seemed to be general agreement among all three that Germany should be divided into an unspecified number of states. Marshal Stalin was of the opinion that the Germans in surrendering should be told about this plan. Mr. Churchill suggested that the questions involved were so complex that further study should be made. The President then suggested that the Foreign Ministers study the matter and submit recommendations within the next thirty days.

At the later meeting in London, in which Ambassador John G. Winant represented the United States, no agreement was reached. When Mr. Hopkins saw Marshal Stalin late in May it was apparent that the Soviet leader had changed his views and had reached the conclusion

that we and the British were opposed to dismemberment. He said it was evident there was no agreement at Yalta; and that at the London meeting the British had interpreted the Crimean discussions to represent not a positive plan but something to hold over Germany's head in case of bad behavior. He suggested that the matter be discussed at the forthcoming meeting of the Big Three at Potsdam. By the time that meeting occurred, however, the thinking of all three governments had veered away from dismemberment and the issue did not arise.

During all the consideration of the German question at Yalta, reparations were the chief interest of the Soviet delegation.

At the conference table Marshal Stalin sat between Mr. Molotov and I. M. Maisky, Deputy Commissar for Foreign Affairs. Maisky had served as the Russian Ambassador in London for eleven years, and at Yalta often acted as interpreter as well as adviser to Stalin. It was he who presented the Soviet proposal on German reparations.

"Our plan foresees that reparations in kind should be demanded from Germany in two ways," Mr. Maisky explained. "First, withdrawals from the national wealth of Germany. That means factories, land, machinery, machine tools, rolling stock of railways, investments in foreign enterprises, and so on. Second, yearly payments in kind after the war in the course of ten years."

He proposed that 80 per cent of all German industry should be withdrawn, specifying the iron and steel, engineering, metal and chemical industries. He added that aviation plants, facilities for the production of synthetic oil and all other military enterprises and factories should be withdrawn entirely.

"By withdrawal I mean to confiscate

and carry away physically and use as reparations payments," he emphasized.

Retention of 20 per cent of Germany's heavy industry would be adequate to sustain the country's economic life, he said. All reparations should be terminated within ten years and the removal of factories and other wealth should be completed in two years. German enterprises important as war potentials should be internationalized with representatives of the three powers sitting on the boards of these enterprises for as many years as the three countries should desire.

Reparations funds should be paid only to those countries that had sustained direct material losses such as damage to factories, land and homes and the losses of personal property by citizens, Mr. Maisky maintained. Because such losses were so huge he proposed that a system of priorities be established among the countries to receive reparations based on their contribution to the winning of the war and the value of their direct material losses.

He then stated that reparations should be fixed at twenty billions of dollars and that the share of the Soviet Union in the reparations fund should not be less than ten billion dollars.

Mr. Churchill responded first to Mr. Maisky's statement. He recalled the experience of the United Kingdom after World War I.

"The process was a very disappointing one," he said. "With great difficulty about 1,000 million pounds was extracted from Germany, and that would never have been extracted if the United States, at the same time, had not loaned Germany a larger sum."

"Removal of plants and factories to a certain extent is a proper step," he declared, "but I am quite sure you will never be able to get out of ruined Germany for Russia alone anything like 215 million pounds a year." He pictured Britain's losses and heavy debts and referred to the severe losses of other countries which must be considered in allotting reparations.

"Secondly," Mr. Churchill continued, "there arises in my mind the specter of an absolutely starving Germany.

"If our treatment of Germany's internal economy is such as to leave eighty million people virtually starving, are we to sit still and say, 'It serves you right,' or will we be required to keep them alive? If so, who is going to pay for that? . . . If you have a horse and you want him to pull the wagon you have to provide him with a certain amount of corn — or at least hay."

"But the horse must not kick you," Mr. Maisky objected.

Mr. Churchill switched to a nonkicking illustration by saying:

"If you have a motorcar you must give it a certain amount of petrol to make it go. I am in favor of having a reparations inquiry committee set up to explore this subject with the object of getting the most we can in a sensible way."

In presenting the position of the United States, President Roosevelt pointed out that after the last war we loaned to Germany billions of dollars, and emphasized "We cannot let that happen again."

"We are in the position of not wanting any of Germany's manpower," the President said. "We do not want any of her machinery, tools, or her factories. There will be some German assets in the United States that might be credited against what Germany owes the United States, but it will amount to very little." After the meeting I advised the President that the best estimate placed the value of German assets in this country at 150 million dollars and that the value certainly would not exceed 200 million. He later used these figures to point out what an exceedingly small amount we would receive in contrast to other nations.

The American people want the Germans to live, the President told the conference, but do not want them to have a higher standard of living than other states, such as the Soviet Republic. He stressed that the United States would emerge from the war in poor financial condition and that we would have no money to send into Germany for food, clothing or housing.

"All I can say is that we will do the best we can in an extremely bad situation," the President said, and concluded by adding we would support the creation of a reparations commission as proposed by the Soviet Union.

Marshal Stalin then entered the discussion. "The root of the trouble the last time," he asserted, "was that reparations were demanded in money. Then, the question arose of transferring the German mark into foreign currencies. That was the rock upon which reparations broke down."

Marshal Stalin urged that the three powers that carried the burden of the war should have priority in reparations. He said it must be admitted that "France did not have any sacrifice to compare to the three powers I have in mind." And then to clinch the argument, he said, "France at this time has in the war eight divisions while the Lublin government has ten divisions." There is no doubt that his opinion as to the claims of a government was influenced by the number of its divisions. He is credited with having said at Yalta, when reference was made to the views of the Pope, "How many divisions does he have?" The Marshal did not make that statement at Yalta.

But it was the yardstick he frequently used.

Stalin concluded his statement with a proposal that a decision be made as to whether reparations should be based upon the contributions made in the prosecution of the war or upon the losses sustained, or whether both should be considered. During the discussion, the President made a statement which still remains a source of misunderstanding between ourselves and the Russians. He said the Reparations Commission "should take, in its initial studies as a basis for discussion, the suggestion of the Soviet government, that the total sum of reparations should be twenty billions and that fifty per cent of it should go to the Soviet Union."

This language was later incorporated in the Conference Protocol, the document prepared by a committee appointed to set forth in writing the agreements reached during a conference. The protocol, which on the last day of the conference was submitted to the heads of government for final approval, also contained the statement that the Reparations Commission could consider "the use of labor" as a possible source of reparations. There was no discussion of this proposal at the conference table except a passing reference by the President in which he said the United States "cannot take manpower as the Soviet Republics can." Later I learned the language was added by Mr. Maisky, the Soviet representative, and subsequently agreed to by the other delegations. At any rate, I did not know of it at the time I left Yalta. Had I known it, I would have urged the President to oppose the inclusion in the protocol of any provision for the use of large groups of human beings as enforced or slave laborers. The program later drafted by the

Reparations Commission contained no provision for "the use of labor." But I regret to say that Germans and Japanese still are being held in Allied hands for use as laborers.

In the days that followed Yalta, as our armies fought their way into Germany from the east and the west, and as our combined air power and artillery pounded the cities of Germany into rubble, it became fully apparent there was no adequate answer to Prime Minister Churchill's contention that Germany would be unable to reimburse the Allies for all the losses inflicted on the people in the various Allied countries. . . .

In October 1943, Secretary of State Cordell Hull had taken with him to Moscow the first proposal that finally developed into the Dumbarton Oaks plan for a United Nations organization. He and the President believed it would be far easier to obtain agreement on a plan for a peace organization while the war was still in progress. How right they were!

At the conclusion of the Dumbarton Oaks Conference, in the autumn of 1944, the only major point remaining at issue was the formula for voting in the Security Council. The Soviet delegation had insisted that all decisions in the Security Council must be by a unanimous vote on the part of the major powers. We agreed that no decision committing our military forces to action should be taken without our consent but did not believe the right of veto should extend to all matters.

We finally had devised a compromise formula which we hoped the Soviets could be persuaded to accept, and the President sent it direct to Marshal Stalin on December 5. At the same time, the State Department prepared and delivered to the Soviet and British embassies in Washington lengthy statements in explanation and support of the President's proposal.

We sought to meet the Soviet insistence that the votes of the five permanent members of the Security Council must be unanimous on all questions by suggesting that Paragraph 3 in the section of the plan dealing with voting procedure in the Security Council should state that unanimity would be required for all categories of decisions except one: in those decisions involving promotion of peaceful settlement of disputes, a permanent member of the council would not cast a vote if it were party to the dispute in question. Such cases, we believed, would be quasi-judicial in character and no nation should be placed above the law in an organization based on the principle of equality under the law. Where the decisions might require the use of force, we felt justified in placing the permanent members in a special position, since they would have to bear the principal responsibility for such action.

It was on the second day of the conference that Secretary Stettinius formally presented our proposal, and the President then asked for its immediate consideration. In supporting the plan, the President referred to the agreement reached at Teheran in which the three heads of government declared: "We recognize fully that supreme responsibility resting upon us and all the United Nations to make a peace that will command the good will of the overwhelming mass of the peoples of the world and banish the scourge and terror of war for many generations."

Conflicting reports of the exchange that followed were presented in the Security Council of the United Nations in the spring of 1947 by the Soviet and the British representatives during a discussion of the veto power and its relationship to the control of atomic energy. Because of this, and because the veto power has remained one of the most controversial issues of the United Nations structure, it may be of interest to present here the major portion of my shorthand record of the views expressed on the veto issue at Yalta.

Since the United States, as the author of the proposal, had clearly stated its position, the exchange was almost entirely between Prime Minister Churchill and Marshal Stalin. It follows:

PRIME MINISTER. The peace of the world depends upon the lasting friendship of the three great powers, but His Majesty's Government feel we should be putting ourselves in a false position if we put ourselves in the position of trying to rule the world when our desire is to serve the world and preserve it from a renewal of the frightful horrors which have fallen upon the mass of its inhabitants. We should make a broad submission to the opinion of the world within the limits stated. We should have the right to state our case against any case stated by the Chinese, for instance, in the case of Hongkong. There is no question that we could not be required to give back Hongkong to the Chinese if we did not feel that was the right thing to do. On the other hand, I feel it would be wrong if China did not have an opportunity to state its case fully. In the same way, if Egypt raises a question against the British affecting the Suez Canal, as has been suggested, I would submit to all the procedure outlined in this statement. I would do this without fear because British rights would be preserved under paragraph 3 when our veto would kill action if we chose to use it.

I presume, Mr. President, if Argentina raises a question against the United States, that the United States will submit to all the procedure of the last five paragraphs and would not vote on the issue. However, the United States could raise its fundamental objections in respect to all the measures to be taken under paragraph 3. . . .

His Majesty's Government see no danger from their point of view in associating themselves with the proposals of the United States. We see great advantage in the three great powers not assuming the position of rulers of all of the rest of the world without even allowing them to state their case. It would not be right for us with the great power we possess to take that position, denying them the right to state their case, and to have measures taken to adjust difficulties short of the powers set out in paragraph 3, on which powers we rely if we are not convinced by our friends and colleagues on the Security Council.

THE MARSHAL. I would like to have this document to study because it is difficult on hearing it read to come to any conclusion. I think that the Dumbarton Oaks decisions have, as an objective, not only to secure to every nation the right to express its opinion, but if any nation should raise a question about some important matter, it raises the question in order to get a decision in the matter. I am sure none of those present would dispute the right of every member of the Assembly to express his opinion.

Mr. Churchill thinks that China, if it raised the question of Hongkong, would be content only with expressing opinion here. He may be mistaken. China will demand a decision in the matter and so would Egypt. Egypt will not have much pleasure in expressing an opinion that the Suez Canal should be returned to Egypt, but would demand a decision on the matter. Therefore, the matter is much more serious than merely expressing an opinion. Also, I would like to ask Mr. Churchill to name the power which may intend to dominate the world. I am sure Great Britain does not want to dominate the world. So one is removed from suspicion. I am sure the United States does not wish to do so, so another is excluded from the powers having intentions to dominate the world.

MR. CHURCHILL. May I answer?

THE MARSHAL. In a minute. When will the great powers accept the provisions that would absolve them from the charge that they intend to dominate the world? I will study the document. At this time it is not very clear to me. I think it is a more serious question than the right of a power to express its intentions or the desire of some power to dominate the world.

PRIME MINISTER. I know that under the leaders of the three powers as represented here we may feel safe. But these leaders may not live forever. In ten years' time we may disappear. A new generation will come which did not experience the horrors of war and may probably forget what we have gone through. We would like to secure the peace for at least fifty years. We have now to build up such a status, such a plan, that we can put as many obstacles as possible to the coming generation quarreling among themselves.

THE MARSHAL. I think that the task is to secure our unity in the future, and, for this purpose, we must agree upon such a covenant as would best serve that purpose. The danger in the future is the possibility of conflicts among ourselves. If there be unity, then the danger from Germany will not be great. Now we have to think how we can create a situation where the three powers here represented, and China —

PRIME MINISTER. — and France.

THE MARSHAL. Yes, and we will keep a united front. I must apologize to the conference. I have been very busy with other matters and had no chance to study this question in detail. As far as I understand what was said in the American proposal, all conflicts are being divided into two categories — conflicts which demand sanctions of a military nature; the other category includes conflicts which could be regulated by peaceful means without military sanctions. Then I understand that, in the consideration of conflicts of both kinds, it is contemplated there should be first a free discussion of the conflict. I understand, also, that in considering the disputes of the first category, which demand military sanctions, that a permanent member being a party to the dispute has a right to vote. But in conflicts of the second category, which could be regulated by peace-

ful means, and do not require sanctions, the party in dispute is not allowed to vote.

We are accused of attaching too great importance to the procedure "how to vote." We are guilty. We attach great importance to the question of voting. All questions are decided by votes and we are interested in the decisions and not in the discussions. Suppose China is a permanent member and demands Hongkong be returned to her. I can assure Mr. Churchill that China will not be alone. They will have some friends in the Assembly. That would be true of Egypt in the case mentioned.

PRIME MINISTER. I could say "no." I would have a right to say that the powers of the World Security Organization could not be used against us if we remained unconvinced.

THE MARSHAL. There is another danger. My colleagues in Moscow cannot forget the case which occurred in 1939 during the Russian-Finnish War, when Britain and France used the League of Nations against us and eventually expelled us and isolated us.

THE PRESIDENT. It is entirely satisfactory for the Marshal to have sufficient time to study the proposal.

I was deeply disturbed by the clear evidence that Stalin had not considered or even read our proposal on voting in the Security Council even though it had been sent to him by diplomatic air pouch on December 5. This was February 6, and it occurred to me that if in those sixty-three days he had not familiarized himself with the subject, he could not be greatly interested in the United Nations organization. It was all the more impressive since this certainly was the only proposal on the agenda with which he was not entirely familiar. My concern remained even though at the next day's meeting Mr. Molotov announced the Soviet Union's acceptance of our proposal, which was later adopted in substantially the same form at San Francisco. . . .

Immediately after announcing the Soviet Union's acceptance of the President's proposal on voting procedure in the Security Council, Mr. Molotov expressed the hope that Byelorussia, the Ukraine and Lithuania would be admitted to the United Nations. In any event, he said, he hoped the first two would be admitted. Marshal Stalin made a forceful plea in support of the suggestion.

Prime Minister Churchill supported the Soviet request, stating: "My heart goes out to White Russia, bleeding from her wounds while beating down the tyrants."

Not wishing to agree, and yet not wanting to oppose Churchill and Stalin directly while the issue of the international organization was in the balance, the President made this statement: "The British Empire has great populations in its dominions, like Australia, Canada and South Africa. The Soviet Government has great masses of population like the three dominions mentioned. The United States has no colonies but has a large population. Brazil is smaller than the Soviet Union but larger in area than the United States. There are many countries with small population, like Honduras and Liberia. We must study the question of whether any country should be given more than one vote. I do not want to break down the principle of one vote to each nation. Therefore, we can decide on the general plan of a meeting to organize the association and then before the meeting, through the Foreign Secretaries, or at that meeting, we can decide these questions and I will be glad to take them up."

There was no dissent. Because I was strongly opposed to granting the Soviet request, I thought the President had done a good job and that we might hear no more of the proposal. But at the conference table the next afternoon the President began reading a report of the meeting of the Foreign Ministers which had just been handed him and said:

"Paragraph 2 is that it will be for the conference to determine the list of the original members of the organization. At that stage the delegates of the United Kingdom and the United States will support the proposal to admit to original membership two Soviet Socialist republics."

The report was agreed to.

I learned later that at the Foreign Ministers' meeting, Mr. Eden, who wanted to be certain of the admission of all members of the British Commonwealth including India, which was not an independent state, agreed with Mr. Molotov on the votes for Byelorussia and the Ukraine. Mr. Stettinius then also agreed to the arrangement. As the meeting opened, the Secretary advised the President of the action which the President later announced, and the heads of government approved.

I was surprised at the agreement which, in my opinion, was very unwise. After the meeting I urged my view upon the President. I reminded him that before we left Washington he had told a group of Senators that if Stalin proposed granting membership to Byelorussia and the Ukraine, he would insist upon membership for each of our forty-eight states. The truth is, the Soviet republics are no more independent than the states of our Union.

I recalled to him how effectively the opponents of the League of Nations had argued that the British, because of their dominions, would have five votes in the Assembly while we would have but one.

Our people had come to realize that the dominions were independent states and frequently held views different from the United Kingdom, but that was not true of the Soviet republics. I feared the opponents of the United Nations might use the allotment of three votes to the Soviet Union as effectively as the foes of the League had used the argument against the British votes twenty-six years earlier. I urged the President at least to ask that the United States be granted a number of votes equal to those of the Soviet Union. The President feared it was too late but said he would consider it.

I convinced Hopkins that, at the very least, we should secure such an agreement from Stalin and Churchill whether or not we afterward exercised the right. He then joined me in urging the President to withdraw his agreement regarding the two Soviet republics unless Russia agreed the United States also should have three votes. The President finally told us he would present it to Marshal Stalin. On the last day I spent at Yalta, February 10, the President wrote him a letter which stated:

I am somewhat concerned lest it be pointed out that the United States will have only one vote in the Assembly. It may be necessary for me, therefore, if I am to insure wholehearted acceptance by the Congress and people of the United States of our participation in the World Organization, to ask for additional votes in the Assembly in order to give parity to the United States.

I would like to know, before I face this problem, that you perceive no objection and would support a proposal along this line if it is necessary for me to make it at the forthcoming conference.

The following day Marshal Stalin advised the President that he entirely agreed with him that "since the number

of votes for the Soviet Union is increased to three in connection with the inclusion of the Soviet Ukraine and Soviet White Russia among the members of the Assembly, the number of votes for the USA should also be increased.

"The number of votes for the USA might be increased to three as in the case of the Soviet Union and its two basic republics," he said. "If it is necessary I am prepared officially to support this proposal."

President Roosevelt also asked Churchill for his views, and Churchill stated he would support the President in any proposal he made to achieve American equality with other nations.

When I arrived in Washington there was waiting for me in the White House Map Room the following cable:

*For Justice Byrnes from Mr. Hopkins*
THE PRESIDENT HAS RECEIVED COMPLETELY SATISFACTORY REPLIES FROM THE PRIME MINISTER AND MARSHAL STALIN ON ADDITIONAL VOTES TO ACHIEVE PARITY FOR THE UNITED STATES, IF NECESSARY. IN VIEW OF THE FACT THAT NOTHING ON THIS WHOLE SUBJECT APPEARS IN THE COMMUNIQUÉ, THE PRESIDENT IS EXTREMELY ANXIOUS NO ASPECT OF THIS QUESTION BE DISCUSSED EVEN PRIVATELY.

I assumed he had some very good reason for not wishing this matter to be discussed, and I complied with the request.

The President and his advisers concluded not to ask at San Francisco for compliance with the agreement that we have as many votes as were given to Russia. He did not again discuss the subject with me, and I did not know he had changed his mind. I admit that the public opposition to Russia's three votes as against our one was not so great as I had expected. But nevertheless I think we should have insisted at San Francisco on the agreement made at Yalta. I felt then and feel now that the smaller states would have opposed the request of the Soviets and the United States. This course would have been just and it would have resulted in both governments having only one vote. That would have been the best solution.

In granting three votes to the Soviet Union, we established a precedent. The Soviets do not overlook precedents favorable to themselves. At the Peace Conference in Paris, for example, Byelorussia and the Ukraine were members. They will demand membership in every other conference. This means the Soviet Union has three arguments as well as three votes. They never fail to make the three arguments or cast the three votes.

The Paris Peace Conference agreed upon two kinds of recommendations, one requiring only a majority vote, the other requiring a two-thirds vote. The Soviet representatives announced that in the Council of Foreign Ministers they would not consider any recommendation adopted by less than a two-thirds vote.

There were twenty-one members of the peace conference. Therefore, eight votes in opposition to a recommendation would prevent its receiving the two-thirds endorsement. When the Soviets opposed a proposal, it was much easier for them to secure these eight votes because they had three votes to start with. Had the Soviets possessed only one vote, or had the United States been given three votes, as was agreed at Yalta, many of the recommendations which received thirteen votes, one short of two-thirds, would have been adopted.

Another agreement was made at Yalta which was to confront me later. This was the "Top Secret" Protocol in which it was agreed that in return for Soviet participation in the war against Japan, the Kurile Islands would be "handed over" to the Soviet Union. It also provided that "the former rights of Russia violated by the treacherous attack of Japan in 1904 shall be restored," and listed these as the return of the southern half of Sakhalin Island, internationalization of the Port of Dairen, the lease of Port Arthur as a Russian naval base, and joint Russo-Chinese operation of the Chinese Eastern and South Manchurian railroads. The United States was to use its influence to have China agree to that part affecting China's territory.

I did not know of this agreement, but the reason is understandable. At that time I was not Secretary of State. Mr. Stettinius was Secretary.

Because of problems that had arisen in Washington, the President wanted me to return with Admiral King, who was leaving at noon on February 10. We expected the conference would end that evening and that the President would leave the following day. But that afternoon Stalin requested the President to remain one more day. He said they could not conclude their work and he wished to discuss some matter he deemed important. The President complied. The agreement as to the Kurile Islands was reached in private conversations among the Big Three instead of at the conference table, and the protocols, including this one, were signed on February 11. Had I been in Yalta that day it is probable I would have learned of it.

When the President returned, he did not mention it to me and the protocol was kept locked in his safe at the White House. In the early summer I learned that President Roosevelt had undertaken to induce China to make the concessions affecting Port Arthur, Dairen, and the railroad, but it was not until some time after I became Secretary of State that a news story from Moscow caused me to inquire and learn of the full agreement. I presented the matter to President Truman and he requested Admiral Leahy to transfer to the State Department those documents at the White House containing agreements with foreign governments. I wanted to know how many IOU's were outstanding.

In considering the wisdom of these Pacific agreements entered into by President Roosevelt, one should be fair enough to consider the circumstances under which the promises were made. It was six weeks after the serious German counterattack on the western front. Although progress was being made in both the east and the west, neither the President nor anyone else at that time knew how long the Germans could hold out and how many casualties we would suffer before they surrendered. The President had with him at Yalta the Joint Chiefs of Staff. They knew the situation.

The evidence is clear that the agreement was, in great part, a military decision. The military leaders already had their plans for the invasion of Japan under way. They undoubtedly gave the President their estimate of what such an invasion would cost us in human lives with Russia in the war and what the cost would be if Russia were out of the war. They naturally wanted Russia in the war to engage the Japanese armies in the north. But once Stalin knew our plans for invasion were under way, he knew also that we would want his armies and he could demand more for them. Mr. Stalin is not bashful about making demands.

Nor should President Roosevelt be criticized for keeping the agreement secret. The Soviet Union was party to a treaty with Japan and we could not announce Russia's intention to go to war with her. Furthermore, Russia's military strength was then concentrated on the German campaign. Any hint of the agreement would have been an invitation to the Japanese troops on Russia's borders to launch an invasion. It was in the interest of all of us to allow the Soviets ninety days after Germany's surrender to transfer troops from the European front. It is, therefore, quite understandable that both Marshal Stalin and President Roosevelt wished to maintain strict secrecy. . . .

The report of the Yalta Conference was released simultaneously from London, Moscow and Washington on Monday afternoon, February 12. All the Allied nations responded favorably and American public opinion was especially enthusiastic. The Philadelphia *Record* called the conference the "greatest United Nations victory of the war." The New York *Herald Tribune* declared that "the overriding fact" is that the conference "has produced another great proof of Allied unity, strength and power of decision." And *Time Magazine* asserted: "all doubts about the Big Three's ability to co-operate in peace as well as in war seem now to have been swept away."

That was how I felt about it. There is no doubt that the tide of Anglo-Soviet-American friendship had reached a new high. But President Roosevelt had barely returned to American soil when the tide began to ebb.

# Winston Churchill: RUSSIA AND POLAND: THE SOVIET PROMISE

POLAND was discussed at no fewer than seven out of the eight plenary meetings of the Yalta Conference, and the British record contains an interchange on this topic of nearly eighteen thousand words between Stalin, Roosevelt, and myself. Aided by our Foreign Ministers and their subordinates, who also held tense and detailed debate at separate meetings among themselves, we finally produced a declaration which represented both a promise to the world and agreement between ourselves on our future actions. The painful tale is still unfinished and the true facts are as yet imperfectly known, but what is here set down may perhaps contribute to a just appreciation of our efforts at the last but one of the war-time Conferences. The difficulties and the problems were ancient, multitudinous, and imperative. The Soviet-sponsored Lublin Government of Poland, or the "Warsaw" Government as the Russians of all names preferred to call it, viewed the London Polish Government with bitter animosity. Feeling between them had got worse, not better, since our October meeting in Moscow. Soviet troops were flooding across Poland, and the Polish Underground Army was freely charged with the murder of Russian soldiers and with sabotage and attacks on their rear areas and their lines of communication. Both access and information were denied to the Western Powers. In Italy and on the Western Front over 150,000 Poles were fighting valiantly for the final destruction of the Nazi armies. They and many others elsewhere in Europe were eagerly looking forward to the liberation of their country and a return to their homeland from voluntary and honourable exile. The large community of Poles in the United States anxiously awaited a settlement between the three Great Powers.

The questions which we discussed may be summarized as follows:

How to form a single Provisional Government for Poland.

How and when to hold free elections.

How to settle the Polish frontiers, both in the east and the west.

How to safeguard the rear areas and lines of communication of the advancing Soviet armies.

The reader should bear in mind the important correspondence between the President and Stalin, and my share in it, about Poland, which is set forth in an earlier chapter. Poland had indeed been the most urgent reason for the Yalta Conference, and was to prove the first of the great causes which led to the breakdown of the Grand Alliance.

When we met on February 6 President Roosevelt opened the discussion by saying that, coming from America, he had a distant view on the Polish question. There were five or six million Poles in the United States, mostly of the second generation, and most of them were gen-

The selections from Winston Churchill, *Triumph and Tragedy*, are reprinted by permission of and arrangement with Houghton Mifflin Company, the authorized publishers.

erally in favour of the Curzon Line. They knew they would have to give up East Poland. They would like East Prussia and part of Germany, or at any rate something with which to be compensated. As he had said at Teheran, it would make it easier for him if the Soviet Government would make some concession such as Lvov, and some of the oil-bearing lands, to counterbalance the loss of Konigsberg. But the most important point was a permanent Government for Poland. General opinion in the United States was against recognising the Lublin Government, because it represented only a small section of Poland and of the Polish nation. There was a demand for a Government of national unity, drawn perhaps from the five main political parties.

He knew none of the members of either the London or Lublin Governments. He had been greatly impressed by Mikolajczyk when he had come to Washington, and felt he was an honest man. He therefore hoped to see the creation of a Government of Poland which would be representative, and which the great majority of Poles would support even if it was only an interim one. There were many ways in which it might be formed, such as creating a small Presidential Council to take temporary control and set up a more permanent institution.

I then said it was my duty to state the position of His Majesty's Government. I had repeatedly declared in Parliament and in public my resolution to support the claim of the U.S.S.R. to the Curzon Line as interpreted by the Soviet Government. That meant including Lvov in the U.S.S.R. I had been considerably criticised in Parliament (as had the Foreign Secretary) and by the Conservative Party for this. But I had always thought that, after the agonies Russia had suffered in

defending herself against the Germans, and her great deeds in driving them back and liberating Poland, her claim was founded not on force but on right. If however she made a gesture of magnanimity to a much weaker Power, and some territorial concession, such as the President had suggested, we should both admire and acclaim the Soviet action.

But a strong, free, and independent Poland was much more important than particular territorial boundaries. I wanted the Poles to be able to live freely and live their own lives in their own way. That was the object which I had always heard Marshal Stalin proclaim with the utmost firmness, and it was because I trusted his declarations about the sovereignty, independence, and freedom of Poland that I rated the frontier question as less important. This was dear to the hearts of the British nation and the Commonwealth. It was for this that we had gone to war against Germany — that Poland should be free and sovereign. Everyone knew what a terrible risk we had taken when we had gone to war in 1939 although so ill-armed. It had nearly cost us our life, not only as an Empire but as a nation. Great Britain had no material interest of any kind in Poland. Honour was the sole reason why we had drawn the sword to help Poland against Hitler's brutal onslaught, and we could never accept any settlement which did not leave her free, independent, and sovereign. Poland must be mistress in her own house and captain of her own soul. Such freedom must not cover any hostile design by Poland or by any Polish group, possibly in intrigue with Germany, against Russia; but the World Organisation that was being set up would surely never tolerate such action or leave Soviet Russia to deal with it alone.

At present there were two Governments of Poland, about which we differed. I had not seen any of the present London Government of Poland. We recognised them, but had not sought their company. On the other hand, Mikolajczyk, Romer, and Grabski were men of good sense and honesty, and with them we had remained in informal but friendly and close relations. The three Great Powers would be criticised if they allowed these rival Governments to cause an apparent division between them, when there were such great tasks in hand and they had such hopes in common. Could we not create a Government or governmental instrument for Poland, pending full and free elections, which could be recognised by all? Such a Government could prepare for a free vote of the Polish people on their future constitution and administration. If this could be done we should have taken one great step forward towards the future peace and prosperity of Central Europe. I said I was sure that the communications of the Russian Army, now driving forward in victorious pursuit of the Germans, could be protected and guaranteed.

After a brief adjournment Stalin spoke. He said that he understood the British Government's feeling that Poland was a question of honour, but for Russia it was a question both of honour and security; of honour because the Russians had had many conflicts with the Poles and the Soviet Government wished to eliminate the causes of such conflicts; of security, not only because Poland was on the frontiers of Russia, but because throughout history Poland had been a corridor through which Russia's enemies had passed to attack her. During the last thirty years the Germans had twice passed through Poland. They passed through because Poland had been weak.

Russia wanted to see a strong and powerful Poland, so that she would be able to shut this corridor of her own strength. Russia could not keep it shut from the outside. It could only be shut from the inside by Poland herself, and it was for this reason that Poland must be free, independent, and powerful. This was a matter of life and death for the Soviet State. Their policy differed greatly from that of the Czarist Government. The Czars had wanted to suppress and assimilate Poland. Soviet Russia had started a policy of friendship, and friendship moreover with an independent Poland. That was the whole basis of the Soviet attitude, namely, that they wanted to see Poland independent, free, and strong.

He then dealt with some of the points which Mr. Roosevelt and I had put forward. The President, he said, had suggested there should be some modification of the Curzon Line and that Lvov and perhaps certain other districts should be given to Poland, and I had said that this would be a gesture of magnanimity. But the Curzon Line had not been invented by the Russians. It had been drawn up by Curzon and Clemenceau and representatives of the United States at the conference in 1919, to which Russia had not been invited. The Curzon Line had been accepted against the will of Russia on the basis of ethnographical data. Lenin had not agreed with it. He had not wished to see the town and province of Bialystok given to Poland. The Russians had already retired from Lenin's position, and now some people wanted Russia to take less than Curzon and Clemenceau had conceded. That would be shameful. When the Ukrainians came to Moscow they would say that Stalin and Molotov were less trustworthy defenders of Russia than Curzon or Clemenceau. It was better that the war should continue a little longer, although it would cost Russia much blood, so that Poland could be compensated at Germany's expense. When Mikolajczyk had been in Russia during October he had asked what frontier for Poland Russia would recognise in the West, and he had been delighted to hear that Russia thought that the western frontier of Poland should be extended to the Neisse. There were two rivers of that name, said Stalin, one near Breslau, and another farther west. It was the Western Neisse he had in mind, and he asked the Conference to support his proposal. . . .

That evening the President wrote a letter to Stalin, after consultation with and amendment by us, urging that two members of the Lublin Government and two from London or from within Poland should come to the Conference and try to agree in our presence about forming a Provisional Government which we could all recognise to hold free elections as soon as possible. I favoured this course, and supported the President when we met again on February 7. Mr. Roosevelt once more emphasised his concern. Frontiers, he said, were important, but it was quite within our province to help the Poles to set up a united temporary Government, or even to set one up ourselves until they could produce one of their own founded on free elections. "We ought to do something," he said, "that will come like a breath of fresh air in the murk that exists at the moment on the Polish question." He then asked Stalin if he would like to add anything to what he had said the day before.

Stalin replied that he had received the President's letter only about an hour and a half before, and had immediately given instructions for Bierut and Morawski to be found so that he could talk to them on the telephone. He had just learned that

they were in Cracow and Lodz respectively, and he promised to ask them how representatives from the opposition camp could be traced, as he did not know their addresses. In case there might not be time to get them to the Conference, Molotov had elaborated some proposals which to some extent met the President's suggestions. . . . As for the river Neisse, mentioned in the second of Molotov's proposals, I reminded my hearers that in previous talks I had always qualified the moving of the Polish frontier westward by saying that the Poles should be free to take territory in the West, but not more than they wished or could properly manage. It would be a great pity to stuff the Polish goose so full of German food that it died of indigestion. I was conscious of a large body of opinion in Great Britain which was frankly shocked at the idea of moving millions of people by force. A great success had been achieved in disentangling the Greek and Turkish populations after the last war, and the two countries had enjoyed good relations ever since; but in that case under a couple of millions of people had been moved. If Poland took East Prussia and Silesia as far as the Oder, that alone would mean moving six million Germans back to Germany. It might be managed, subject to the moral question, which I would have to settle with my own people.

Stalin observed that there were no Germans in these areas, as they had all run away.

I replied that the question was whether there was room for them in what was left of Germany. Six or seven million Germans had been killed and another million (Stalin suggested two millions) would probably be killed before the end of the war. There should therefore be room for these migrant people up to a certain point. They would be needed to fill the

vacancies. I was not afraid of the problem of transferring populations, so long
as it was proportionate to what the Poles
could manage and to what could be put
into Germany. But it was a matter which
required study, not as a question of principle, but of the numbers which would
have to be handled.

In these general discussions maps were
not used, and the distinction between
the Eastern and Western Neisse did not
emerge as clearly as it should have
done. This was however soon to be made
clear. . . .

When we met again on February 8
Mr. Roosevelt read out his revised proposals based on Molotov's draft. "No
objection," he stated, "is perceived to the
Soviet proposal that the eastern boundary of Poland should be the Curzon
Line, with modifications in favour of
Poland in some areas of from five to eight
kilometres." Here at least was one matter on which we could all agree, and
although I had invited the Russians to
make some minor concessions it seemed
better not to multiply our difficulties,
which were already serious enough. But
the President was firm and precise about
the frontier in the west. He agreed that
Poland should receive compensation at
the expense of Germany, "including that
portion of East Prussia south of the
Konigsberg line, Upper Silesia, and up to
the line of the Oder; but," he continued,
*"there would appear to be little justifica-
tion for extending it up to the Western
Neisse."* This had always been my view,
and I was to press it very hard when we
met again at Potsdam five months later.

There remained the question of forming a Polish Government which we could
all recognise and which the Polish nation
would accept. Mr. Roosevelt suggested
a Presidential Committee of three Polish
leaders who would go to Moscow, form

a Provisional Government from representatives in Warsaw, London, and inside
Poland itself, and hold free elections as
soon as possible.

After a short adjournment Molotov
voiced his disagreement. The Lublin
Government, he said, was now at the
head of the Polish people. It had been
enthusiastically acclaimed by most of
them and enjoyed great authority and
prestige. The same could not be said of
the men from London. If we tried to
create a new Government the Poles
themselves might never agree so it was
better to try to enlarge the existing one.
It would only be a temporary institution,
because all our proposals had but one
object, namely, to hold free elections in
Poland as soon as possible. How to enlarge it could best be discussed in Moscow between the American and British
Ambassadors and himself. He said he
greatly desired an agreement, and he
accepted the President's proposals to invite two out of the five people mentioned
in his letter of February 6. There was
always the possibility, he said, that the
Lublin Government would refuse to talk
with some of them, like Mikolajczyk, but
if they sent three representatives and two
came from those suggested by Mr. Roosevelt conversations could start at once.

"What about the Presidential Committee?" asked Mr. Roosevelt.

"Better avoid it," he answered. "It
will mean having two bodies to deal with
instead of one."

"This," I said, "is the crucial point of
the Conference. The whole world is waiting for a settlement, and if we separate
still recognising different Polish Governments the whole world will see that fundamental differences between us still
exist. The consequences will be most
lamentable, and will stamp our meeting
with the seal of failure. On the other

hand of course we take different views about the basic facts in Poland, or at any rate some of them. According to British information, the Lublin Government does not commend itself to the great majority of the Polish people, and we cannot feel that it would be accepted abroad as representing them. If the Conference is to brush aside the existing London Government and lend all its weight to the Lublin Government there will be a world outcry. As far as can be foreseen, the Poles outside of Poland will make a virtually united protest. There is under our command a Polish army of 150,000 men, who have been gathered from all who have been able to come together from outside Poland. This army has fought, and is still fighting, very bravely. I do not believe it will be at all reconciled to the Lublin Government, and if Great Britain transfers recognition from the Government which it has recognised since the beginning of the war they will look on it as a betrayal.

"As Marshal Stalin and M. Molotov well know," I proceeded, "I myself do not agree with the London Government's action, which has been foolish at every stage. But the formal act of transferring recognition from those whom we have hitherto recognised to this new Government would cause the gravest criticism. It would be said that His Majesty's Government have given way completely on the eastern frontier (as in fact we have) and have accepted and championed the Soviet view. It would also be said that we have broken altogether with the lawful Government of Poland, which we have recognised for these five years of war, and that we have no knowledge of what is actually going on in Poland. We cannot enter the country. We cannot see and hear what opinion is. It would be said we can only accept what the Lublin Government proclaims about the opinion of the Polish people, and His Majesty's Government would be charged in Parliament with having altogether forsaken the cause of Poland. The debates which would follow would be most painful and embarrassing to the unity of the Allies, even supposing that we were able to agree to the proposals of my friend M. Molotov.

"I do not think," I continued, "that these proposals go nearly far enough. If we give up the Polish Government in London a new start should be made from both sides on more or less equal terms. Before His Majesty's Government ceased to recognise the London Government and transferred their recognition to another Government they would have to be satisfied that the new Government was truly representative of the Polish nation. I agree that this is only one point of view, as we do not fully know the facts, and all our differences will of course be removed if a free and unfettered General Election is held in Poland by ballot and with universal suffrage and free candidatures. Once this is done His Majesty's Government will salute the Government that emerges without regard to the Polish Government in London. It is the interval before the election that is causing us so much anxiety."

Molotov said that perhaps the talks in Moscow would have some useful result. It was very difficult to deal with this question without the participation of the Poles themselves, who would have to have their say. I agreed, but said that it was so important that the Conference should separate on a note of agreement that we must all struggle patiently to achieve it. The President supported me. He said that it was the great objective of the Americans that there should be an early General Election in Poland. The only problem was how the country was to be governed in the meantime, and he hoped it would be possible to hold elections before the end of the year. The problem was therefore limited in time.

Stalin now took up my complaint that I had no information and no way of getting it.

"I have a certain amount," I replied.

"It doesn't agree with mine," he answered, and proceeded to make a speech, in which he assured us that the Lublin Government was really very popular, particularly Bierut, Osobka-Morawski, and General Zymierski. They had not left the country during the German occupation, but had lived all the time in Warsaw and came from the underground movement. That made a deep impression on the Poles, and the peculiar mentality of people who had lived under the German occupation should be borne in mind. They sympathised with all those who had not left the country in difficult times, and they considered the three persons he had named to be people of that kind. He said he did not believe that they were geniuses. The London Government might well contain cleverer people, but they were not liked in Poland because they had not been seen there when the population was suffering under the Hitlerite occupation. It was perhaps a primitive feeling, but it certainly existed.

It was, he said, a great event in Poland that the country had been liberated by Soviet troops, and this had changed everything. It was well known that the Poles had not liked the Russians, because they had three times helped to partition Poland. But the advance of the Soviet troops and the liberation of Poland had completely changed their mood. The old resentment had disappeared, and had given way to goodwill and even enthusiasm for the Russians. That was perfectly natural. The population had been delighted to see the Germans flee and to feel that they were liberated. Stalin said it was his impression that the Polish population considered the driving out of the Germans a great patriotic holiday in Polish life, and they were astonished that the London Government did not take any part in this festival of the Polish nation. They saw on the streets the members of the Provisional Government, but asked where were the London Poles. This undermined the prestige of the London Government, and was the reason why the Provisional Government, though not great men, enjoyed great popularity.

Stalin thought that these facts could not be ignored if we wanted to understand the feelings of the Polish people. I had said that I feared the Conference separating before agreement was reached. What then was to be done? The various Governments had different information, and drew different conclusions from it. Perhaps the first thing was to call together the Poles from the different camps and hear what they had to say.

There was dissatisfaction, he continued, because the Polish Government was not elected. It would naturally be better to have a Government based on free elections, but the war had so far prevented that. But the day was near when elections could be held. Until then we must deal with the Provisional Government, as we had dealt, for instance, with General de Gaulle's Government in France, which also was not elected. He did not know whether Bierut or General de Gaulle enjoyed greater authority, but it had been possible to make a treaty with General de Gaulle, so why could we not do the same with an enlarged Polish Government, which would be no less democratic? It was not reasonable to demand more from Poland than from

France. So far the French Government had carried out no reform which created enthusiasm in France, whereas the Polish Government had enacted a land reform which had aroused great enthusiasm. If we approached the matter without prejudice we should be able to find common ground. The situation was not as tragic as I thought, and the question could be settled if too much importance was not attached to secondary matters and if we concentrated on essentials.

"How soon," asked the President, "will it be possible to hold elections?"

"Within a month," Stalin replied, "unless there is some catastrophe on the front, which is improbable."

I said that this would of course set our minds at rest, and we could wholeheartedly support a freely elected Government which would supersede everything else, but we must not ask for anything which would in any way hamper the military operations. These were the supreme ends. If however the will of the Polish people could be ascertained in so short a time, or even within two months, the situation would be entirely different and no one could oppose it.

We thereupon agreed to let our Foreign Secretaries talk the matter over.

The three Ministers accordingly met at noon on February 9. They were unable to agree. When however the Conference assembled in plenary session at four o'clock in the afternoon Molotov produced some fresh proposals which were much nearer to the American draft. The Lublin Government was to be "reorganised on a wider democratic basis, with the inclusion of democratic leaders from Poland itself, and also from those living abroad." He and the British and American Ambassadors should consult together in Moscow about how this would be done. Once reorganised the Lublin Gov-

ernment would be pledged to hold free elections as soon as possible, and we should then recognise whatever Government emerged. Mr. Stettinius had desired a written pledge that the three Ambassadors in Warsaw should observe and report that the elections were really free and unfettered, but Molotov opposed this, because, he alleged, it would offend the Poles. Subject to this and to a few minor amendments, he accepted the United States plan.

This was a considerable advance, and I said so, but I felt it my duty to sound a general warning. This would be the last but one of our meetings. There was an atmosphere of agreement, but there was also a desire to put foot in the stirrup and be off. We could not, I declared, afford to allow the settlement of these important matters to be hurried and the fruits of the Conference lost for lack of another twenty-four hours. A great prize was in view and decisions must be unhurried. These might well be among the most important days in our lives.

Mr. Roosevelt declared that the differences between us and the Russians were now largely a matter of words, but both he and I were anxious that the elections should really be fair and free. I told Stalin that we were at a great disadvantage, because we knew so little of what was going on inside Poland and yet had to take decisions of great responsibility. I knew, for instance, that there was bitter feeling among the Poles and that M. Osubka-Morawski had used very fierce language, and I had been told that the Lublin Government had openly said it would try as traitors all members of the Polish Home Army and underground movement. This, I said, caused me anxiety and distress. Of course I put the security of the Red Army first, but I begged Stalin to consider our difficulty.

The British Government did not know what was going on inside Poland, except through dropping brave men by parachute and bringing members of the underground movement out. We had no other means of knowing, and did not like getting our information in this way. How could this be remedied without in any way hampering the movements of the Soviet troops? Could any facilities be granted to the British (and no doubt to the United States) for seeing how these Polish quarrels were being settled? Tito had said that when elections took place in Yugoslavia he would not object to Russian, British, and American observers being present to report impartially to the world that they had been carried out fairly. So far as Greece was concerned, His Majesty's Government would greatly welcome American, Russian, and British observers to make sure the elections were conducted as the people wished. The same question would arise in Italy. When Northern Italy was delivered there would be a vast change in the Italian political situation, and there would have to be an election before it was possible to form a Constituent Assembly or Parliament. The British formula there was the same — Russian, American, and British observers should be present to assure the world that everything had been done in a fair way. It was impossible, I said, to exaggerate the importance of carrying out elections fairly. For instance, would Mikolajczyk be able to go back to Poland and organise his party for the elections?

"That will have to be considered by the Ambassadors and M. Molotov when they meet the Poles," said Stalin.

I replied, "I must be able to tell the House of Commons that the elections will be free and that there will be effec- tive guarantees that they are freely and fairly carried out."

Stalin pointed out that Mikolajczyk belonged to the Peasant Party, which, as it was not a Fascist party, could take part in the elections and put up its candidates. I said that this would be still more certain if the Peasant Party were already represented in the Polish Government, and Stalin agreed that the Government should include one of their representatives.

I said that we should have to leave it at that, and added that I hoped that nothing I had said had given offense, since nothing had been further from my heart.

"We shall have to hear," he answered, "what the Poles have to say."

I explained that I wanted to be able to carry the eastern frontier question through Parliament, and I thought this might be done if Parliament was satisfied that the Poles had been able to decide for themselves what they wanted.

"There are some very good people among them," he replied. "They are good fighters, and they have had some good scientists and musicians, but they are very quarrelsome."

"All I want," I answered, "is for all sides to get a fair hearing."

"The elections," said the President, "must be above criticism, like Caesar's wife. I want some kind of assurance to give to the world, and I don't want anybody to be able to question their purity. It is a matter of good politics rather than principle."

"I am afraid," said Molotov, "that if we insert the American draft the Poles will feel they are not trusted. We had better discuss it with them."

I was not content with this, and re- solved to raise it with Stalin later on. The opportunity presented itself next day.

Just before our last effective meeting, on February 10, Mr. Eden and I had a private conversation with Stalin and Molotov at the Yusupov Villa, at which I once more explained how difficult it was for us to have no representatives in Poland who could report what was going on. The alternatives were either an Ambassador with an embassy staff or newspaper correspondents. The latter was less desirable, but I pointed out that I should be asked in Parliament about the Lublin Government and the elections and I must be able to say that I knew what was happening.

"After the new Polish Government is recognized it would be open to you to send an Ambassador to Warsaw," Stalin answered.

"Would he be free to move about the country?"

"As far as the Red Army is concerned, there will be no interference with his movements, and I promise to give the necessary instructions, but you will have to make your own arrangements with the Polish Government."

Stalin also pointed out that de Gaulle had a representative in Poland.

We then agreed to add the following to our declaration:

As a consequence of the above, recognition should entail an exchange of Ambassadors, by whose reports the respective Governments would be informed about the situation in Poland.

This was the best I could get. . . .

At noon on February 27 I asked the House of Commons to approve the results of the Crimea Conference. I said:

I am anxious that all parties should be united in this new instrument, so that these supreme affairs shall be, in Mr. Gladstone's words, "high and dry above the ebb and flow of party politics." . . . The Crimea Conference leaves the Allies more closely united than before, both in the military and in the political sphere. Let Germany ever recognise that it is futile to hope for division among the Allies and that nothing can avert her utter defeat. Further resistance will only be the cause of needless suffering. The Allies are resolved that Germany shall be totally disarmed, that Nazism and militarism in Germany shall be destroyed, that war criminals shall be justly and swiftly punished, that all German industry capable of military production shall be eliminated or controlled, and that Germany shall make compensation in kind to the utmost of her ability for damage done to Allied nations. On the other hand, it is not the purpose of the Allies to destroy the people of Germany, or leave them without the necessary means of subsistence. Our policy is not revenge; it is to take such measures as may be necessary to secure the future peace and safety of the world. There will be a place one day for Germans in the comity of nations, but only when all traces of Nazism and militarism have been effectively and finally extirpated.

Poland was the issue which disturbed the House.

The three Powers are agreed that acceptance by the Poles of the provisions on the eastern frontiers, and, so far as can now be ascertained, on the western frontiers, is an essential condition of the establishment and future welfare and security of a strong, independent, homogeneous Polish State. . . . But even more important than the frontiers of Poland, within the limits now disclosed, is the freedom of Poland. The home of the Poles is settled. Are they to be masters in their own house? Are they to be free, as we in Britain and the United States or France are free? Are their sovereignty and their independence to be untrammelled, or are they to become a mere projection of the Soviet State, forced against their will by an armed minority to adopt a Communist or totalitarian system? I am putting the case in all its bluntness. It is a touchstone far more sensitive and vital than the drawing of frontier lines. Where does Poland stand? Where do we all stand on this?

Most solemn declarations have been made by Marshal Stalin and the Soviet Union that the sovereign independence of Poland is to be maintained, and this decision is now joined in both by Great Britain and the United States. Here also the World Organisation will in due course assume a measure of responsibility. The Poles will have their future in their own hands, with the single limitation that they must honestly follow, in harmony with their Allies, a policy friendly to Russia. That is surely reasonable. . . .

The agreement provides for consultations, with a view to the establishment in Poland of a new Polish Provisional Government of National Unity, with which the three major Powers can all enter into diplomatic relations, instead of some recognising one Polish Government and the rest another. . . . His Majesty's Government intend to do all in their power to ensure that . . . representative Poles of all democratic parties are given full freedom to come and make their views known.

I felt bound to proclaim my confidence in Soviet good faith in the hope of procuring it. In this I was encouraged by Stalin's behaviour about Greece.

The impression I brought back from the Crimea, and from all my other contacts, is that Marshal Stalin and the Soviet leaders wish to live in honourable friendship and equality with the Western democracies. I feel also that their word is their bond. I know of no Government which stands to its obligations, even in its own despite, more solidly than the Russian Soviet Government. I decline absolutely to embark here on a discussion about Russian good faith. It is quite evident that these matters touch the whole future of the world. Sombre indeed would be the fortunes of mankind if some awful schism arose between the Western democracies and the Russian Soviet Union.

I continued:

We are now entering a world of imponderables, and at every stage occasions for self-questioning arise. It is a mistake to look too far ahead. Only one link in the chain of destiny can be handled at a time.

I trust the House will feel that hope has been powerfully strengthened by our meeting in the Crimea. The ties that bind the three Great Powers together and their mutual comprehension of each other have grown. The United States has entered deeply and constructively into the life and salvation of Europe. We have all three set our hands to far-reaching engagements at once practical and solemn. . . .

The general reaction of the House was unqualified support for the attitude we had taken at the Crimea Conference. There was however intense moral feeling about our obligations to the Poles, who had suffered so much at German hands and on whose behalf as a last resort we had gone to war. A group of about thirty Members felt so strongly on this matter that some of them spoke in opposition to the motion which I had moved. There was a sense of anguish lest we should have to face the enslavement of a heroic nation. Mr. Eden supported me. In the division on the second day we had an overwhelming majority, but twenty-five Members, most of them Conservatives, voted against the Government, and in addition eleven members of the Government abstained. Mr. H. G. Strauss, who was Parliamentary Secretary to the Ministry of Town and Country Planning, resigned.

It is not permitted to those charged

with dealing with events in times of war or crisis to confine themselves purely to the statement of broad general principles on which good people agree. They have to take definite decisions from day to day. They have to adopt postures which must be solidly maintained, otherwise how can any combinations for action be maintained? It is easy, after the Germans are beaten, to condemn those who did their best to hearten the Russian military effort and to keep in harmonious contact with our great Ally, who had suffered so frightfully. What would have happened if we had quarrelled with Russia while the Germans still had two or three hundred divisions on the fighting front? Our hopeful assumptions were soon to be falsified. Still, they were the only ones possible at the time.

# *Robert E. Sherwood*: THE YALTA CONFERENCE

NONE of the momentous conferences of the Second World War has provoked more subsequent controversy than this one; Yalta has been blamed for many of the ills with which the world was afflicted in the years following the total defeat of Nazi Germany and Japan. The belief has grown that Roosevelt made various "surrenders" to the Russians at Yalta, and the more kindly critics attribute these to the fact that he was a dying man. The complete records of the Conference, as they appear in the Hopkins papers, do not seem to substantiate this theory. Roosevelt appears to have been in full possession of all of his faculties. Only at the end of seven days of long meetings, covering a wide range of tremendous subjects, did he make a concession which, in my belief, he would not have made if he had not been tired out and anxious to end the negotiations relative to Russia's entry into the war with Japan. This will be discussed later in this chapter. Of all the "surrenders" supposed to have been made, those most often cited and emphasized relate to the establishment of the veto power in the Security Council of the United Nations and the granting to the Soviet Union of two additional votes in the General Assembly. These two points have often been linked together under the general term, "the voting formula," but they were entirely separate problems and the first of them was not a subject of contention at Yalta. . . .

There is no doubt that Roosevelt had come to Yalta determined to oppose the Russian demand for the two additional votes. In fact, it is my understanding that he had previously told the Cabinet and Congressional leaders in Washington that if the Russians were to insist on this point he would demand forty-eight votes for the United States. Now, at Yalta, Churchill spoke out strongly in favor of the admission of the two republics. I do not know what his reasons were for this, but it seemed evident to the Americans present that he was influenced by British imperial considerations and especially the problem of India.

When the Foreign Secretaries' meeting

considered the issue the following day, Eden supported Molotov, and Stettinius reserved his position. It was agreed, however, that only those countries which had signed the United Nations Declaration by the day on which the Yalta Conference should end would be invited to the San Francisco Conference. Subsequently, in view of the British unwillingness to join him in objecting to the two extra votes, Roosevelt decided to agree to support the Russian proposal at San Francisco but insisted that it must be a matter for full discussion and free vote at the later conference and not a *fait accompli* at Yalta. . . .

The question of the Russian claim for reparations in kind from Germany was argued back and forth throughout the Yalta Conference. Both Churchill and Roosevelt said that public opinion in their countries was opposed to the whole concept of reparations in view of the unfortunate results of the Treaty of Versailles — and Stalin was later to confess to Hopkins that he became pretty fed up with hearing about American and British public opinion, believing that the President and Prime Minister kept on referring to it merely as a device to justify their own personal opinions and prejudices. The Russians never did succeed in understanding that public opinion could be a determining factor even with the powerful heads of state; Stalin had said to Roosevelt at Teheran that the way to overcome the moral objections of the American people to absorption of the Baltic States in the Soviet Union was to subject them to a propaganda campaign, and Vishinski had expressed precisely the same point of view in his remark to Bohlen that the American people should learn to obey their leaders.

In the final meeting at Yalta, the whole question of reparations seemed to have reached a deadlock. It was decided that the matter should be referred to an Inter-allied Commission to be set up in Moscow, but it seemed impossible to agree on the terms of the basic directive on which this Commission would proceed. During the argument, Hopkins wrote the following note and passed it to Roosevelt: "The Russians have given in so much at this conference that I don't think we should let them down. Let the British disagree if they want to — and continue their disagreement at Moscow. Simply say it is all referred to the Reparations Commission with the minutes to show the British disagree about any mention of the 10 billion." Roosevelt took that advice, believing he had left the door open for all sorts of deliberations in the future. . . .

At Yalta, Roosevelt was adhering to the basic formula of unconditional surrender; beyond that, he demanded only — to quote one of his favorite phrases — "freedom of action." Therefore, when he said that the Reparations Commission should "in its initial studies" take the Soviet suggestion in regard to reparations "as a basis for discussion," it may be assumed that he meant precisely what he said and no more. . . .

. . . The decisive discussions (they are all on the record) relative to the Far East and Russia's entry into the war against Japan were conducted between Roosevelt and Stalin with Churchill not present, although he joined in signing the final written agreement which has been the subject of so much controversy since its terms were made public.

In *Where Are We Heading?* Sumner Welles has offered serious criticism of elements in this agreement. Welles saw no valid objection to the return of southern Sakhalin and the Kurile Islands to Russia, since these positions, which the

Japanese had seized, were highly important and even essential to Russian security in the Far East; nor was there objection to the internationalization of Dairen (provided it ever were truly "internationalized") nor to the granting of permanent autonomy to Outer Mongolia. "However," Welles wrote, "the restoration to Russia of the right formerly possessed by the Imperial Russian Governments to dominate Manchuria through the control of the Chinese Eastern and South Manchurian railroads, and the lease of Port Arthur as a naval base, necessarily fall into a different category. These concessions, which will make it altogether impossible for a new unified China to exercise full sovereignty within Manchuria, are all the more objectionable in view of China's absence from the conference table where they were decided." Such criticism from Welles could hardly be dismissed as coming from one who did not know what he was talking about or who was embittered by hatred of Roosevelt. But it may be said that in writing them Welles had the considerable advantage of hindsight.

It is quite clear that Roosevelt had been prepared even before the Teheran Conference in 1943 to agree to the legitimacy of most if not all of the Soviet claims in the Far East, for they involved the restoration of possessions and privileges taken by the Japanese from the Russians in the war of 1904. It is also clear that the failure to notify the Chinese immediately of the Yalta discussions was due to fear of the security of secrets in Chungking. Stalin told Roosevelt at Yalta that he intended to start the movement of twenty-five Russian divisions across Siberia to the Far East and this operation must be conducted in utmost secrecy, and Roosevelt said that when this movement of troops had been completed (presumably within three or four months) he would send an American officer to Chungking via Moscow to inform Chiang Kai-shek of the agreements. Stalin insisted that these agreements must be put in writing and must contain the statement: "The Heads of the three Great Powers have agreed that these claims of the Soviet Union shall be unquestionably fulfilled after Japan has been defeated."

This, in my opinion, was the most assailable point in the entire Yalta record, and the most surprising in that it involved Roosevelt in the kind of firm commitment that usually he managed to avoid. It denied him the postwar "freedom of action" which he valued so highly; for, if China had refused to agree to any of the Soviet claims, presumably the U. S. and Britain would have been compelled to join in enforcing them.

It must be said that in all considerations of Far Eastern matters at Yalta Roosevelt's principal concern was based on American war plans against Japan. The immensely costly operations at Iwo Jima and then at Okinawa were about to be launched, and the plans had been made for the major invasion of the Japanese home islands in the fall of 1945. MacArthur's calculations were based on the assumption that the Russians would contain the great bulk of Japanese forces on the Asiatic mainland as they had contained the Germans in Eastern Europe. Obviously, the entry of the Soviet Union forcibly into the Japanese war by midsummer — before the major invasion — could mean the saving of countless American lives, and might even make the final invasion unnecessary. Of course, at the time of Yalta, the perfection of the atomic bomb still seemed to be only a remote possibility for the uncertain future; it was not until three months after

Roosevelt's death that assurance came from Los Alamos that the long years of research and experiment on this decisive weapon had achieved success.

In spite of all of which, it is my belief that Roosevelt would not have agreed to that final firm commitment had it not been that the Yalta Conference was almost at an end and he was tired and anxious to avoid further argument. I believe that he was hopeful that, when the time came to notify the Chinese, he would be able to straighten the whole thing out with Chiang Kai-shek — but that hope, of course, was not realized.

During the discussion of the Far Eastern agreements — and there was not much discussion — Stalin said to Roosevelt that if his conditions were not met it would be very difficult to explain to the Russian people why they must go to war against Japan. (Here the Marshal was obviously using the "public opinion" tactic which he complained of when used by Roosevelt or Churchill.) He said that the Russian people had clearly understood that they must fight the Germans to defend the very existence of their homeland, but that they could see no such threat from the Japanese. However, Stalin said, if the required political conditions were met, then it would not be difficult for him to explain to the Supreme Soviet and the people just what was their stake in the Far Eastern war.

Stalin agreed to the establishment of American air bases at Komsomolsk and Nikolaevsk in the near future, and later on Kamchatka, the delay in the latter case being due to the presence there of a Japanese Consul who could not fail to notice the presence of U. S. Air Force personnel. Stalin also agreed to the immediate institution of American-Russian military staff talks for joint planning.

It was agreed that "in two or three months after Germany has surrendered and the war in Europe had terminated the Soviet Union shall enter the war against Japan on the side of the Allies."

Stalin again expressed his lack of confidence in China as a world power. He said that he could not understand why the Kuomintang Government and the Communists should not maintain a united front against the Japanese. He felt that Chiang Kai-shek should assume leadership for this purpose but that there was a need for some new leaders around the Generalissimo. He said there were some good men in the Comintern and he did not understand why they had not been brought forward. (He later restated these views more explicitly in his talks with Hopkins in Moscow.)

Roosevelt said that the new American Ambassador, General Hurley, and General Wedemeyer were much more successful than their predecessors in bringing the Communists in the North together with the Chungking Government. He said that the blame for the breach lay more with the Comintern and the Kuomintang than with the rank and file of the so-called Communists.

Stalin asked Roosevelt whether any foreign troops would be stationed in Korea. Roosevelt replied in the negative, and Stalin expressed his approval of this.

A large dinner was given by Stalin on the evening of February 8 and a smaller one (with only the principals attending) by Churchill on the last evening, February 10. The record of the principal toasts at the former dinner was as follows:

*Marshal Stalin* proposed a toast to the health of the Prime Minister, whom he characterized as the bravest governmental figure in the world. He said that due in large measure to Mr. Churchill's courage and staunchness, England, when she stood alone, had divided the might of Hitlerite Germany at a time when the rest of Europe was falling flat on its face before Hitler. He said that Great Britain, under Mr. Churchill's leadership, had carried on the fight alone irrespective of existing or potential allies. The Marshal concluded that he knew of few examples in history where the courage of one man had been so important to the future history of the world. He drank a toast to Mr. Churchill, his fighting friend and a brave man.

*The Prime Minister,* in his reply, toasted Marshal Stalin as the mighty leader of a mighty country, which had taken the full shock of the German war machine, had broken its back and had driven the tyrants from her soil. He said he knew that in peace no less than in war Marshal Stalin would continue to lead his people from success to success.

*Marshal Stalin* then proposed the health of the President of the United States. He said that he and Mr. Churchill in their respective countries had had relatively simple decisions. They had been fighting for their very existence against Hitlerite Germany but there was a third man whose country had not been seriously threatened with invasion, but who had had perhaps a broader conception of national interest and even though his country was not directly imperilled had been the chief forger of instruments which had led to the mobilization of the world against Hitler. He mentioned in this connection Lend-Lease as one of the President's most remarkable and vital achievements in the formation of the Anti-Hitler combination and in keeping the allies in the field against Hitler.

*The President,* in reply to this toast, said he felt the atmosphere at this dinner was as that of a family, and it was in those words that he liked to characterize the relations that existed between our three countries. He said that great changes had occurred in the world during the last three years, and even greater changes were to come. He said that each of the leaders represented here were working in their own way for the interests of their people. He said that fifty years ago there were vast areas of the world where people had little opportunity and no hope, but much had been accomplished, although there were still great areas where people had little opportunity and little hope, and their objectives here were to give to every man, woman and child on this earth the possibility of security and well being.

In a subsequent toast to the alliance between the three great powers, *Marshal Stalin* remarked that it was not so difficult to keep unity in time of war since there was a joint aim to defeat the common enemy which was clear to everyone. He said the difficult task came after the war when diverse interests tended to divide the Allies. He said he was confident that the present alliance would meet this test also and that it was our duty to see that it would, and that our relations in peacetime should be as strong as they had been in war.

*The Prime Minister* then said he felt we were all standing on the crest of a hill with the glories of future possibilities stretching before us. He said that in the modern world the function of leadership was to lead the people out from the forests into the broad sunlit plains of peace and happiness. He felt this prize was nearer our grasp than anytime before in history and it would be a tragedy for which history would never forgive us if we let this prize slip from our grasp through inertia or carelessness.

The mood of the American delegates, including Roosevelt and Hopkins, could be described as one of supreme exultation as they left Yalta. They were confident that their British colleagues agreed with them that this had been the most encouraging conference of all, and the immediate response of the principal spokesmen for British and American public opinion added immeasurably to their sense of satisfaction with the job that had been done. As soon as Roosevelt came on board the *Quincy* on Great Bitter Lake (so ominously and perhaps so appropriately named) he received floods of messages telling of the enthusiastic response to the publication of the Yalta communiqués in the United States. One of the cables quoted Herbert Hoover as saying, "It will offer a great hope to the world." William L. Shirer called it "a landmark in human history." Raymond Gram Swing said, "No more appropriate news could be conceived to celebrate the birthday of Abraham Lincoln." Senator Barkley cabled, "Accept my sincere felicitations upon the historic Joint Statement released today. I had it read to the Senate immediately upon release and it made a profound impression. Senator White, Minority Leader, joined me in the expressions of commendation and satisfaction on the floor of the Senate. I regard it as one of the most important steps ever taken to promote peace and happiness in the world."

Joseph C. Harsch wrote, in the *Christian Science Monitor*, "The Crimea Conference stands out from previous such conferences because of its mood of decision. The meetings which produced the Atlantic Charter, Casablanca, Teheran, Quebec — all these were dominated, politically, by declarative moods. They were declarations of policy, of aspirations, of intents. But they were not meetings of decision. The meeting at Yalta was plainly dominated by a desire, willingness and determination to reach solid decisions."

Hopkins later said to me, "We really believed in our hearts that this was the dawn of the new day we had all been praying for and talking about for so many years. We were absolutely certain that we had won the first great victory of the peace — and, by 'we,' I mean *all* of us, the whole civilized human race. The Russians had proved that they could be reasonable and farseeing and there wasn't any doubt in the minds of the President or any of us that we could live with them and get along with them peacefully for as far into the future as any of us could imagine. But I have to make one amendment to that — I think we all had in our minds the reservation that we could not foretell what the results would be if anything should happen to Stalin. We felt sure that we could count on him to be reasonable and sensible and understanding — but we never could be sure who or what might be in back of him there in the Kremlin."

# THE CRIMEA (YALTA) CONFERENCE

## PROTOCOL OF PROCEEDINGS, FEBRUARY 11, 1945

THE Crimea Conference of the Heads of the Governments of the United States of America, the United Kingdom, and the Union of Soviet Socialist Republics which took place from February 4th to 11th came to the following conclusions:

I. *World Organisation*

It was decided:

(1) that a United Nations Conference on the proposed world organisation should be summoned for Wednesday, 25th April, 1945, and should be held in the United States of America.

(2) the Nations to be invited to this Conference should be:

(a) the United Nations as they existed on the 8th February, 1945; and

(b) such of the Associated Nations as have declared war on the common enemy by 1st March, 1945. (For this purpose by the term "Associated Nations" was meant the eight Associated Nations and Turkey). When the Conference on World Organisation is held, the delegates of the United Kingdom and United States of America will support a proposal to admit to original membership two Soviet Socialist Republics, i.e. the Ukraine and White Russia.

(3) that the United States Government on behalf of the Three Powers should consult the Government of China and the French Provisional Government in regard to decisions taken at the present Conference concerning the proposed World Organisation.

(4) that the text of the invitation to be issued to all the nations which would take part in the United Nations Conference should be as follows:

INVITATION

The Government of the United States of America, on behalf of itself and of the Governments of the United Kingdom, the Union of Soviet Socialist Republics, and the Republic of China and the Provisional Government of the French Republic, invite the Government of _____ to send representatives to a Conference of the United Nations to be held on 25th April, 1945, or soon thereafter, at San Francisco in the United States of America to prepare a Charter for a General International Organisation for the maintenance of international peace and security.

The above named governments suggest that the Conference consider as affording a basis for such a Charter the Proposals for the Establishment of a General International Organisation, which were made public last October as a result of the Dumbarton Oaks Conference, and which have now been supplemented by the following provisions for Section C of Chapter VI:

"C. Voting

"1. Each member of the Security Council should have one vote.

"2. Decisions of the Security Council on procedural matters should be made by an affirmative vote of seven members.

"3. Decisions of the Security Council on all other matters should be made by an affirmative vote of seven members including the concurring votes of the permanent members;

From *Official Documents, Texts of selected documents on US foreign policy 1918–1952* (New York, Woodrow Wilson Foundation, 1952), pp. 10–19.

provided that, in decisions under Chapter VIII, Section A and under the second sentence of paragraph 1 of Chapter VIII, Section C, a party to a dispute should abstain from voting."

Further information as to arrangements will be transmitted subsequently.

In the event that the Government of _____ desires in advance of the Conference to present views or comments concerning the proposals, the Government of the United States of America will be pleased to transmit such views and comments to the other participating Governments.

### TERRITORIAL TRUSTEESHIP

It was agreed that the five Nations which will have permanent seats on the Security Council should consult each other prior to the United Nations Conference on the question of territorial trusteeship.

The acceptance of this recommendation is subject to its being made clear that territorial trusteeship will only apply to (a) existing mandates of the League of Nations; (b) territories detached from the enemy as a result of the present war; (c) any other territory which might voluntarily be placed under trusteeship; and (d) no discussion of actual territories is contemplated at the forthcoming United Nations Conference or in the preliminary consultations, and it will be a matter for subsequent agreement which territories within the above categories will be placed under trusteeship.

## II. *Declaration on Liberated Europe*

The following declaration has been approved:

The Premier of the Union of Soviet Socialist Republics, the Prime Minister of the United Kingdom and the President of the United States of America have consulted with each other in the common interests of the peoples of their countries and those of liberated Europe. They jointly declare their mutual agreement to concert during the temporary period of instability in liberated Europe the policies of their three governments in assisting the peoples of the former Axis satellite states of Europe to solve by democratic means their pressing political and economic problems.

The establishment of order in Europe and the re-building of national economic life must be achieved by processes which will enable the liberated peoples to destroy the last vestiges of Nazism and Fascism and to create democratic institutions of their own choice. This is a principle of the Atlantic Charter — the right of all peoples to choose the form of government under which they will live — the restoration of sovereign rights and self-government to those peoples who have been forcibly deprived of them by the aggressor nations.

To foster the conditions in which the liberated peoples may exercise these rights, the three governments will jointly assist the people in any European liberated state or former Axis satellite state in Europe where in their judgment conditions require (a) to establish conditions of internal peace; (b) to carry out emergency measures for the relief of distressed peoples; (c) to form interim governmental authorities broadly representative of all democratic elements in the population and pledged to the earliest possible establishment through free elections of governments responsive to the will of the people; and (d) to facilitate where necessary the holding of such elections.

The three governments will consult the other United Nations and provisional authorities or other governments in Europe when matters of direct interest to them are under consideration.

When, in the opinion of the three governments, conditions in any European liberated state or any former Axis satellite state in Europe make such action necessary, they will immediately consult together on the measures necessary to discharge the joint responsibilities set forth in this declaration.

By this declaration we reaffirm our faith in the principles of the Atlantic Charter, our pledges in the Declaration by the United Nations, and our determination to build in co-operation with other peace-loving nations world order under law, dedicated to peace, security, freedom and general well-being of all mankind.

In issuing this declaration, the Three Powers express the hope that the Provisional Government of the French Republic may be associated with them in the procedure suggested.

### III. *Dismemberment of Germany*

It was agreed that Article 12 (a) of the Surrender Terms for Germany should be amended to read as follows:

The United Kingdom, the United States of America and the Union of Soviet Socialist Republics shall possess supreme authority with respect to Germany. In the exercise of such authority they will take such steps, including the complete disarmament, de-militarisation and dismemberment of Germany as they deem requisite for future peace and security.

The study of the procedure for the dismemberment of Germany was referred to a Committee, consisting of Mr. Eden (Chairman), Mr. Winant and Mr. Gousev. This body would consider the desirability of associating with it a French representative.

### IV. *Zone of Occupation for the French and Control Council for Germany*

It was agreed that a zone in Germany, to be occupied by the French Forces, should be allocated to France. This zone would be formed out of the British and American zones and its extent would be settled by the British and Americans in consultation with the French Provisional Government.

It was also agreed that the French Pro-visional Government should be invited to become a member of the Allied Control Council of Germany.

### V. *Reparation*

THE HEADS of the three governments agreed as follows:

1. Germany must pay in kind for the losses caused by her to the Allied nations in the course of the war. Reparations are to be received in the first instance by those countries which have borne the main burden of the war, have suffered the heaviest losses and have organised victory over the enemy.

2. Reparation in kind to be exacted from Germany in three following forms:

(a) Removals within 2 years from the surrender of Germany or the cessation of organised resistance from the national wealth of Germany located on the territory of Germany herself as well as outside her territory (equipment, machine-tools, ships, rolling stock, German investments abroad, shares of industrial, transport and other enterprises in Germany etc.), these removals to be carried out chiefly for purpose of destroying the war potential of Germany.

(b) Annual deliveries of goods from current production for a period to be fixed.

(c) Use of German labour.

3. For the working out on the above principles of a detailed plan for exaction of reparation from Germany an Allied Reparation Commission will be set up in Moscow. It will consist of three representatives — one from the Union of Soviet Socialist Republics, one from the United Kingdom and one from the United States of America.

4. With regard to the fixing of the total sum of the reparation as well as the dis-

tribution of it among the countries which suffered from the German aggression the Soviet and American delegations agreed as follows:

The Moscow Reparation Commission should take in its initial studies as a basis for discussion the suggestion of the Soviet Government that the total sum of the reparation in accordance with the points (a) and (b) of the paragraph 2 should be 20 billion dollars and that 50% of it should go to the Union of Soviet Socialist Republics.

The British delegation was of the opinion that pending consideration of the reparation question by the Moscow Reparation Commission no figures of reparation should be mentioned.

The above Soviet-American proposal has been passed to the Moscow Reparation Commission as one of the proposals to be considered by the Commission.

## VI. *Major War Criminals*

The Conference agreed that the question of the major war criminals should be the subject of enquiry by the three Foreign Secretaries for report in due course after the close of the Conference.

## VII. *Poland*

The following Declaration on Poland was agreed by the Conference:

A new situation has been created in Poland as a result of her complete liberation by the Red Army. This calls for the establishment of a Polish Provisional Government which can be more broadly based than was possible before the recent liberation of Western part of Poland. The Provisional Government which is now functioning in Poland should therefore be reorganised on a broader democratic basis with the inclusion of democratic leaders from Poland itself and from Poles abroad. This new Government should then be

called the Polish Provisional Government of National Unity.

M. Molotov, Mr. Harriman and Sir A. Clark Kerr are authorised as a commission to consult in the first instance in Moscow with members of the present Provisional Government and with other Polish democratic leaders from within Poland and from abroad, with a view to the reorganisation of the present Government along the above lines. This Polish Provisional Government of National Unity shall be pledged to the holding of free and unfettered elections as soon as possible on the basis of universal suffrage and secret ballot. In these elections all democratic and anti-Nazi parties shall have the right to take part and to put forward candidates.

When a Polish Provisional Government of National Unity has been properly formed in conformity with the above, the Government of the U.S.S.R., which now maintains diplomatic relations with the present Provisional Government of Poland, and the Government of the United Kingdom and the Government of the United States of America will establish diplomatic relations with the new Polish Provisional Government of National Unity, and will exchange Ambassadors by whose reports the respective Governments will be kept informed about the situation in Poland.

The three Heads of Government consider that the Eastern frontier of Poland should follow the Curzon Line with digressions from it in some regions of five to eight kilometres in favour of Poland. They recognise that Poland must receive substantial accession of territory in the North and West. They feel that the opinion of the new Polish Provisional Government of National Unity should be sought in due course on the extent of these accessions and that the final delimitation of the Western frontier of Poland should thereafter await the Peace Conference.

## VIII. *Yugoslavia*

It was agreed to recommend to Marshal Tito and to Dr. Subasic:

(a) that the Tito-Subasic Agreement

should immediately be put into effect and a new Government formed on the basis of the Agreement

(b) that as soon as the new Government has been formed it should declare:

(i) that the Anti-Fascist Assembly of National Liberation (·Aunoj) will be extended to include members of the last Yugoslav Skupstina who have not compromised themselves by collaboration with the enemy, thus forming a body to be known as a temporary Parliament and

(ii) that legislative acts passed by the Anti-Fascist Assembly of National Liberation (Aunoj) will be subject to subsequent ratification by a Constituent Assembly; and that this statement should be published in the Communiqués of the Conference.

## IX. *Italo-Yugoslav Frontier*
### *Italo-Austria Frontier*

Notes on these subjects were put in by the British delegation and the American and Soviet delegations agreed to consider them and give their views later.

## X. *Yugoslav-Bulgarian Relations*

There was an exchange of views between the Foreign Secretaries on the question of the desirability of a Yugoslav-Bulgarian pact of alliance. The question at issue was whether a state still under an armistice régime could be allowed to enter into a treaty with another state. Mr. Eden suggested that the Bulgarian and Yugoslav Governments should be informed that this could not be approved. Mr. Stettinius suggested that the British and American Ambassadors should discuss the matter further with M. Molotov in Moscow. M. Molotov agreed with the proposal of Mr. Stettinius.

## XI. *Southeastern Europe*

The British Delegation put in notes for the consideration of their colleagues on the following subjects:

(a) the Control Commission in Bulgaria

(b) Greek claims upon Bulgaria, more particularly with reference to reparations

(c) Oil equipment in Rumania

## XII. *Iran*

Mr. Eden, Mr. Stettinius and M. Molotov exchanged views on the situation in Iran. It was agreed that this matter should be pursued through the diplomatic channel.

## XIII. *Meetings of the Three Foreign Secretaries*

The Conference agreed that permanent machinery should be set up for consultation between the three Foreign Secretaries; they should meet as often as necessary, probably about every three or four months.

These meetings will be held in rotation in the three capitals, the first meeting being held in London.

## XIV. *The Montreux Convention and the Straits*

It was agreed that at the next meeting of the three Foreign Secretaries to be held in London, they should consider proposals which it was understood the Soviet Government would put forward in relation to the Montreux Convention and report to their Governments. The Turkish Government should be informed at the appropriate moment.

The foregoing Protocol was approved and signed by the three Foreign Secretaries at the Crimean Conference, February 11, 1945.

E. R. STETTINIUS, JR.
M. MOLOTOV
ANTHONY EDEN

## AGREEMENT REGARDING JAPAN, FEBRUARY 11, 1945

The leaders of the three Great Powers — the Soviet Union, the United States of America and Great Britain — have agreed that in two or three months after Germany has surrendered and the war in Europe has terminated the Soviet Union shall enter into the war against Japan on the side of the Allies on condition that:

1. The status quo in Outer-Mongolia (The Mongolian People's Republic) shall be preserved;

2. The former rights of Russia violated by the treacherous attack of Japan in 1904 shall be restored, viz:

(a) the southern part of Sakhalin as well as all the islands adjacent to it shall be returned to the Soviet Union,

(b) the commercial port of Dairen shall be internationalized, the preeminent interests of the Soviet Union in this port being safeguarded and the lease of Port Arthur as a naval base of the U.S.-S.R. restored,

(c) the Chinese-Eastern Railroad and the South-Manchurian Railroad which provides an outlet to Dairen shall be jointly operated by the establishment of a joint Soviet-Chinese Company, it being understood that the preeminent interests of the Soviet Union shall be safeguarded and that China shall retain full sovereignty in Manchuria;

3. The Kurile islands shall be handed over to the Soviet Union. It is understood, that the agreement concerning Outer-Mongolia and the ports and railroads referred to above will require concurrence of Generalissimo Chiang Kai-Shek. The President will take measures in order to obtain this concurrence on advice from Marshal Stalin.

The Heads of the three Great Powers have agreed that these claims of the Soviet Union shall be unquestionably fulfilled after Japan has been defeated.

For its part the Soviet Union expresses its readiness to conclude with the National Government of China a pact of friendship and alliance between the U.S.S.R. and China in order to render assistance to China with its armed forces for the purpose of liberating China from the Japanese yoke.

JOSEPH V. STALIN
FRANKLIN D. ROOSEVELT
WINSTON S. CHURCHILL
*February 11, 1945*

# G. F. Hudson: THE LESSON OF YALTA

ONLY nine years have passed since the Yalta Conference, but already it seems an enormously long time ago. The photographs of the Big Three seated together appear today to belong to as remote a past as representations of Pharaohs on the walls of Egyptian temples or figures in the Bayeux Tapestry. It is difficult indeed now to recapture the atmosphere of those far-off days when,

From "The Lesson of Yalta" by G. F. Hudson, *Commentary*, April 1954, with the permission of American Jewish Committee.

as Robert Sherwood tells us in *The White House Papers of Harry L. Hopkins:*

The mood of the American delegates, including Roosevelt and Hopkins, could be described as one of supreme exultation as they left Yalta. They were confident that their British colleagues agreed with them that this had been the most encouraging conference of all, and the immediate response of the principal spokesmen for British and American public opinion added immeasurably to their sense of satisfaction with the job that had been done.

If in 1954 there are few people who can see cause for satisfaction, and still less for exultation, in what was done at Yalta, it has to be remembered that we have the advantage of hindsight and there is always force in the proverb that it is easy to be wise after the event. Certainly there are some politicians who today most loudly condemn the Yalta decisions, but were hardly conspicuous in protest at the time. On the other hand, account must also be taken of the fact that the American and British governments had at their disposal information which was not then available to the general public or even to Congressmen and Members of Parliament — information which pointed very definitely to the long-term aims of Soviet policy. The historian who would arrive at a fair estimate of the Yalta record must try to avoid being prejudiced by the experience of the years since February 1945, but he must at the same time ask how far the hopes set on Yalta were reasonable in the light of the evidence the Western statesmen then already had before their eyes.

The case on their behalf was recently made, though not without substantial concessions to the critics, in an editorial of the *New York Times* (January 24, 1954):

Yalta was a wartime conference at which some good agreements, some bad agreements, and some indifferent agreements were made. It was a grievous error that the whole of these agreements was not public or at least communicated to the Senate. It was a grievous error to promise the Soviet Union rights that belonged to the Nationalist Government of China. But Yalta was also a prelude to the United Nations; at Yalta Russia agreed with the other conferees on free elections with secret ballot in Poland and other lands plundered by the Nazis. If Russia had honorably and honestly carried out its part of the agreement, Yalta might be remembered with reasonable satisfaction. In any case there is every reason to suppose that under the circumstances that existed in early 1945 the Senate would have ratified the Yalta understanding for what then seemed to be the supremely important purpose of getting Soviet Russia into the war against Japan.

Three points are made in this argument: first, that some of the agreements made at Yalta were harmless, or even beneficial; second, that the agreements about Poland and other East European countries were in themselves just and only went wrong because of violations by Russia; and third, that the agreement about China was justified — or would at least have been endorsed by the Senate — because of the imperative need for inducing Russia to join in the war against Japan. The first of these points cannot be taken very seriously. The charge against the Western statesmen is, to put it briefly, that they yielded to Russia the sovereign rights of two allied nations, Poland and China, without the consent of their recognized governments, thereby violating the principles on which the policy of the Western Powers was supposed to be based and facilitating the expansion of Communist power which has been the great disaster of the postwar period. In relation to this charge it is irrelevant to plead that Russia was at the same time persuaded to join the United Nations or to permit France to participate in the military occupation of Germany, just as it would be unhelpful for a man accused of murder to try to extenuate his crime by saying that on the same day that he killed his victim he also contributed generously to the funds of his local church.

Even if the various Yalta agreements are regarded as a single whole in which concessions were traded each way, it would still remain a matter for condemnation that the leaders of the Western democracies treated the sovereignties of their allies as diplomatic trading assets. If these acts are to be justified at all, it must be by showing either that the vital interests of Poland and China were somehow safeguarded, at any rate on paper, or else that their sacrifice was required by overwhelming military necessity in the struggle against Germany and Japan.

On Poland, Harry Hopkins has recorded, in notes of a conversation between Roosevelt, Eden, and himself as far back as March 1943, that "the President said that, after all, the big powers would have to decide what Poland should have, and that he, the President, did not intend to go to the Peace Conference and bargain with Poland or the other small states; as far as Poland is concerned, the important thing is to set it up in a way that will help maintain the peace of the world." This attitude was curiously similar to that advocated in the same month by the Soviet Ambassador, who told Hopkins that "he felt that Great Britain and the United States should decide what was to be done about Poland and 'tell them' rather than ask them."

This talk of Great Power dictation to Poland was less than two years after the promulgation of the Atlantic Charter, in which Roosevelt and Churchill had declared it to be their policy to restore sovereignty to countries that had been deprived of it by the war. Already, it seems, wartime habits had inclined the President towards a distinctly arrogant and peremptory attitude towards weaker Allied nations, which was in striking contrast to his desire to soothe and conciliate the Soviet Union. By November of 1944, three months before the Yalta Conference, his views on the Polish question are thus recorded by Arthur Bliss Lane, who had an interview with him after being appointed American Ambassador to Poland:

I observed that the Soviet view of an independent Poland was quite different from our conception. The President stated that he had entire confidence in Stalin's word and he felt sure that he would not go back on it. I said that I regretted I could not agree with him, as Stalin's previous actions had shown him not to be dependable. . . . Mr. Roosevelt said that he thought Stalin's idea of having a *cordon sanitaire* in the shape of a Poland under Russian influence, as a bulwark to protect the Soviet Union . . . was understandable; Stalin himself had pointed out to the President that after World War I the Allies had formed a *cordon sanitaire* . . . to protect them from the threat of Bolshevism and now he claimed a corresponding right to protect himself from the West.

Roosevelt was apparently unable to see that there was no valid analogy between the so-called *cordon sanitaire* of the years after World War I and what Stalin was doing in Poland in the autumn of 1944. It is true that in the former period the states along the western border of the Soviet Union — Finland, the Baltic States, and Poland, which had been formed in whole or in part from the territory of the old Russian empire, together with Rumania, which had annexed Bessarabia — had an intense fear and distrust of the new Communist Russia and were regarded by conservative politicians in Western Europe as a convenient barrier against the westward expansion of Soviet power. But their governments were not imposed on them by French or British military occupation, and far from being obedient satellites, they often acted in a manner of which London and Paris strongly disapproved. Stalin, on the other hand, having invaded and seized half the territory of Poland in 1939 in alliance with Nazi Germany and deported some 10 per cent of its population to Arctic Russia, Siberia, and Central Asia, had now in 1944 placed Russian-occupied Poland under the rule of a group of Polish Communists and their stooges, while the NKVD imprisoned or executed supporters of the Polish government-in-exile which had been recognized by the United States and Britain as legally representing the Polish state ever since the joint German-Russian conquest of the country.

Roosevelt must have been well aware of this situation, but he preferred to indulge his private vision of a postwar world controlled by a benevolent directorate of Great Powers — a fancy in which he was encouraged by amateur and unofficial advisers. Warned of Stalin's ambitions of European domination, he replied: "I just have a hunch that Stalin isn't that kind of a man. Harry tells me he's not and that he doesn't want anything but security for his country. I think that if I give him everything I possibly can and ask for nothing in return, he won't try to annex anything and will work with me for a world of peace and democracy."

It is clear that if Roosevelt was thus convinced that Stalin wanted nothing but security for his country, and if he found it so "understandable" that Stalin claimed a Poland "under Russian influence" as his *cordon sanitaire,* he could have no strong objection to Soviet nomination of Polish cabinet ministers as a means of insuring this influence. Indeed, had it not been for the agitation carried on in the United States by the Polish-American Congress and a certain restiveness in Congress, it seems doubtful whether Roosevelt would have made any difficulty at all about transferring diplomatic recognition to the Lublin Committee in its original form. Certainly he did not feel himself restrained from so doing by any considerations of international law, for during the Yalta Conference, according to Stettinius, who is not a hostile witness, he declared that "he did not attach much importance to the continuity or legality of any Polish Government, since he felt that for some years there had been in reality no Polish Government." In comment on this astonishing statement it is only necessary to point out that since September 1939 President Roosevelt's administration had concluded several formally signed treaties with the government which he claimed at Yalta had never really existed.

Churchill's attitude to Poland was widely different from Roosevelt's, and yet in practice it converged with his towards the same outcome of surrender to Russian demands. Where Roosevelt saw Stalin as a just and good man who only wanted security for his country, Churchill saw him as an irresistible conqueror of Eastern Europe and held that only by abject submission to his demands could the Poles expect to retain even a fraction of their independence. In Moscow, in October 1944, he told Romer, the Foreign Minister of the Polish government-in-exile, that "Poland is threatened with virtual extinction and would be effaced as a nation" unless the Polish government agreed forthwith to cede to the Soviet Union nearly a half of Poland's pre-war territory and amalgamate with the Lublin Committee, the latter's terms for the coalition being that the Communists should have three-quarters of the Cabinet seats, including control of the army and police.

Churchill's attitude was a strictly "realist" one; the Poles were faced with overwhelming force, and nobody was in a position to help them, so they must submit in the hope of obtaining some mitigation of the conqueror's terms. But Churchill's pressure on the Polish government to capitulate to Russia was not inspired by any illusions about Communism; on the contrary, Churchill was very much aware of the Communist menace in Europe at a time when the American government was totally blind to it, and he did not hesitate to oppose it wherever he had military force available. In November 1944 British troops were used to turn back Communist armed bands marching on Brussels for a *coup d'etat* (similar Communist plans in France having been forestalled by the action of General de Gaulle); in Athens in December, British opposition to seizure of power by the Greek Communists led to severe and prolonged fighting.

There was no support from Washington for these anti-Communist moves; the British intervention in Greece evoked a storm of criticism in the American press and the official attitude was adverse to it. In spite of the lack of American cooperation, Churchill succeeded in preventing Communist domination of Greece — which would have involved the encirclement and subjugation of Turkey as well — but he was only able to obtain a free hand in Greece as far as Russia was concerned by an agreement recognizing similar Russian rights of temporary administration in Rumania and Bulgaria. Although Poland was not specifically included in this demarcation of zones of influence, it was implied that the Russians could arrange matters as they pleased where they had actual military occupation, and thereafter it was difficult to reassert any general principles applicable to all European countries. In saving Greece, Churchill had in effect written off the rest of Eastern Europe.

The memoirs of Stettinius bear witness to the pessimism of Churchill just before the Yalta Conference. Of his meeting with Churchill at Malta on the way to the Crimea, Stettinius writes:

During the course of conversation Churchill expressed utter dismay at the outlook of the world. He said that there were probably more units of suffering among humanity as of this hour, while we were meeting, than ever before in history. As he looked out in the world, he added, it was one of sorrow and bloodshed. It was his opinion that future peace, stability, and progress depended on Great Britain and the United States remaining in close harmony at all times.

The pessimism of Churchill, however, worked against the cause of Polish independence no less than the optimism of Roosevelt did. The only difference was that, whereas Roosevelt could see no harm in a Soviet *cordon sanitaire* covering Eastern Europe, Churchill regarded it as an evil which could not be prevented. Moreover, his resolve not to get out of step with America if he could avoid it inclined him to give way on issues combining Roosevelt and Stalin against him.

Shortly before the Yalta meeting, and in spite of a personal appeal from Roosevelt not to take such action before the conference, Stalin had formally recognized the Communist-controlled Lublin Committee as the *de jure* government of Poland. As both the United States and Britain still recognized the Polish government-in-exile in London — which had the allegiance of all the Polish armed forces operating in Western Europe — the Soviet move was a provocative challenge to them and they could not simply transfer recognition to the puppet régime without appearing to submit to Soviet pressure. There was enough sympathy and support for Poland both in America and in Britain to make it politically risky for the American and British governments to accept the Russian *fait accompli* in Poland unless they could present to their own peoples some appearance of having reached a compromise on the subject. They must be able plausibly to claim that they had not recognized the Lublin Committee, but had got Russia to agree to a new coalition government.

This, however, was only a matter of show for domestic consumption in America and Britain. The deeper political issue was whether the American and British leaders could in fact do anything to alter the situation created by Russian policy and restore the national independence of Poland. They had one high card to play — their power to grant or withhold recognition. Since Poland was under Russian military occupation, they could not directly intervene there, but they could declare that they would not transfer diplomatic recognition from the Polish government-in-exile to any newly created Polish authority until free elections had been held in Poland to ascertain the wishes of the Polish people.

Such a stand would have put Stalin in a dilemma, for he would either have to allow free elections — which, as he well

knew, would give his puppets only a small minority of the votes cast — or dispense indefinitely with Western recognition for the régime he had set up in Poland. That he attached importance to Western recognition, in spite of his own monopoly of force in Poland, was shown by the intensity of the diplomatic pressure he brought to bear on the Western statesmen to accord it.

His armies had overrun vast areas of Eastern Europe outside the pre-war boundaries of the Soviet Union and were followed by the terrorist detachments of the NKVD; everywhere they had the aid of groups of local Communists with a miscellaneous following of dupes, opportunists, and adventurers. But they were faced with the massive hostility of popular feeling which relied on the moral support of the Western Allies against Russian domination and hoped for better times when the war was over. To break the passive resistance of the conquered peoples, to reduce them to apathy and despair, and to turn their sentiments against the West, Stalin needed Western recognition of his puppet governments, and particularly the abandonment of that unsubdued Polish national leadership which had directed the heroic resistance of Poland to Nazi conquest ever since the beginning of the war.

If Roosevelt and Churchill had seriously hoped or intended to restore the independence of Poland, they would have made the transfer of diplomatic recognition to a new Polish government conditional on the actual holding of free elections in Poland, not on a mere promise to hold them. Instead they agreed, in a document which made no mention of the Polish government with which they were still in diplomatic relations, that "the Provisional Government which is now functioning in Poland (i.e. the

Lublin Committee) should be recognized on a broader democratic basis with the inclusion of democratic leaders from Poland itself and from Poles abroad"; that this "reorganized" government "shall be pledged to the holding of free and unfettered elections as soon as possible on the basis of universal suffrage and secret ballot"; and that the government thus pledged should be recognized forthwith by the three Great Powers without waiting for the elections to be held. The government which after long negotiations was eventually formed and recognized by America and Britain as fulfilling the terms of the Yalta agreement kept a majority of the cabinet seats for ex-members of the Lublin Committee and retained the key ministries of Public Security and Defense — with control of the police and army respectively — in Communist hands, while the Soviet citizen Bierut was left as head of the Polish state.

The elections which were to have been held "as soon as possible" were not held until January 1947, and then they were rigged by the Communists with every conceivable device of violence, intimidation, and fraud. By that time, however, the Polish Communist régime had enjoyed the fruits of *de jure* recognition for a year and a half, and the shameless violation of the pledge on condition of which it had originally been recognized did not cause either the American or the British government to withdraw its ambassador from Warsaw.

It must be emphasized that the Big Three at Yalta did not guarantee free elections in Poland or undertake any responsibility for supervising them; they only required a pledge of free elections from the Polish Communists. In view of the violence and terror which then already prevailed in Poland, it is incredible that any Western statesman or diplomat could seriously have believed that such a pledge was of any value without some machinery for supervision to which Russia would be legally committed. But Russia was not committed to anything. The Polish Communists alone gave the pledge and they alone broke it; the Big Three bore no formal responsibility in the matter.

The agreement on Poland and the effect subsequently given to it deprived of all significance the high-sounding generalizations of the "Declaration on Liberated Europe" which was also signed at Yalta. The principles enunciated in this declaration were admirable, but nobody in Eastern Europe could expect that they would be applied otherwise than according to the precedent of what had been done in Poland. If the Western Powers had accepted the accomplished fact of a Soviet puppet régime in Poland without insisting on previous elections or on more than an ineffective minority representation for non-Communist parties in the government, what reason was there to anticipate that they could or would do more for Rumania or Hungary or Czechoslovakia or Bulgaria? The Yalta decisions necessarily broke the back of opposition to Communist rule, not only in Poland, but in every country that had been or was about to be overrun by Russian armies.

What, then, can be urged in justification of the agreement? Why were the Western Powers in such a hurry to recognize a new Polish government before elections could be held? It is sometimes argued that, with the war against Hitler still unfinished, the Western Allies could not afford to quarrel with Stalin. But neither could he afford to quarrel with them. He could not simply withdraw from the war, because unless he got his army into Germany, he could not take the war booty and reparations which were to be the spoils of victory. The Western Allies were in sufficient strength on the Rhine to go to Berlin without him if necessary. As far as Europe was concerned, the Big Three could hardly avoid finishing the war together, whatever their diplomatic differences. But Roosevelt may have felt that nothing must be done to annoy Stalin lest it cause him to refuse to join in the war against Japan. If that was the explanation, Poland must be added to the concessions made at Yalta at the expense of China specifically, as the price for Russian aid in the Pacific war.

The section of the Yalta agreement relating to Manchuria has been the most widely criticized of all the Yalta decisions. Like the agreement on Poland, it was a deal between the Big Three to the detriment of a weaker Allied nation and without its consent. But it differed from the Polish "solution" in two important respects. In the first place, whereas Poland was already under Russian occupation, so that the only question was whether an accomplished fact could be altered, the concessions of Chinese sovereign rights to Russia referred to the future and were promised to Russia as a reward for prospective entry into the Pacific war. Second, while in all the negotiations on European questions both Roosevelt and Churchill took part, together with their respective Foreign Ministers, Roosevelt negotiated the agreement for Russia's entry into the Pacific war not only without consulting Churchill (who was only invited to sign it after it had been concluded), but also without the participation of his own Secretary of State.

The exclusion of Stettinius from this transaction is indeed the most extraordinary feature of the whole Yalta Conference. The excuse was that the agreement

for Russia's entry into the war was purely a military matter in which the State Department was not concerned; Stettinius himself in his memoirs, whether out of loyalty to Roosevelt or to cover up his own humiliation, accepts this version of the matter.

But a treaty involving extensive postwar territorial changes and transfers of sovereign rights is obviously the proper concern of a country's diplomats, not merely of its soldiers.

Moreover, Hopkins and Harriman, who were not military men, were brought into the discussions, though Stettinius and his team of advisers from the State Department were kept out of them. Roosevelt's failure to call on them for information and advice about the extremely complex Far Eastern problems with which he had to deal is all the more strange because he had previously refrained from reading the memoranda which the State Department had prepared for his perusal on the journey to the conference. Byrnes relates in *Speaking Frankly:*

. . . not until the day before we landed at Malta did I learn that we had on board a very complete file of studies and recommendations prepared by the State Department. I asked the President if the Department had given him any material and he advised me it was all in the custody of Lieutenant William M. Rigdon. Later, when I saw some of these splendid studies, I greatly regretted they had not been considered on board ship. I am sure the failure to study them while en route was due to the President's illness. And I am sure that only President Roosevelt, with his intimate knowledge of the problems, could have handled the situation so well with so little preparation.

Roosevelt's own knowledge of the problems, however, appears not to have been as intimate as Byrnes would have us believe. The agreement on Manchuria stated that "the former rights of Russia violated by the treacherous attack of Japan in 1904 shall be restored," and afterwards, in verbal justification of the pact, Roosevelt claimed that the Russians were not getting anything new from China but only recovering what the Japanese had taken from them. This indicates that he was unaware that the original leases to Russia of Port Arthur, Dairen, and the South Manchurian Railway had expired twenty years previously and had only been renewed in favor of Japan as a result of the Japanese "Twenty-one Demands" of 1915, while the Russian rights in the Chinese Eastern Railways, as revised by the Sino-Soviet treaty of 1924, had been voluntarily sold by Russia to Japan over China's vehement protest in 1935.

These were historical facts not likely to be known to anyone who was not a specialist in Far Eastern affairs, and a President of the United States could not be expected to discover them by intuition, but if he had been willing to avail himself of the services of the State Department — which kept files and archives for recording such facts — he would have been correctly informed about the past history of the properties which he so lightly made over to Stalin at China's expense. He would have been informed also that these leased territories and railways, whether held by Russia or Japan, had prevented the proper exercise of Chinese sovereignty in Manchuria for half a century, and that at best he was perpetuating what had hitherto proved to be the most dangerous and intractable source of conflict in Far Eastern affairs.

There can be little doubt that Roosevelt avoided consulting Stettinius about this deal for the same reason that he avoided consulting Churchill or Chiang Kai-shek — because he anticipated that they would object. He did not want to read State Department memoranda because they might not fit in with his intentions. Stalin's terms for entering the Pacific war had already been communicated to Roosevelt before Yalta, and he seems to have made up his mind to grant them without giving his official advisers a chance to discuss them — especially in view of the known opinions of Under Secretary Grew, who had been Ambassador to Japan for ten years and had a great knowledge of Far Eastern problems.

It does not follow, however, that because Roosevelt did not consult the State Department, he did not consult anybody. He had his own executive assistants at the White House, and the one of them specially in charge of Far Eastern affairs was Lauchlin Currie. Currie was mentioned as a fellow-traveler closely connected with the American Communist underground in the list of names given by Whittaker Chambers to Assistant Secretary Adolph Berle in 1940, and was named as a former member of a Soviet spy ring in the recently published FBI report on Communist espionage which was sent to President Truman at the end of 1945. The McCarran Committee also heard considerable testimony about the political activities which Currie is alleged to have carried on in relation to Far Eastern affairs without the knowledge or consent of the State Department. It may be inferred that, if Roosevelt ever asked his advice on what should be conceded to Russia in Manchuria, the advice given would probably not have been to the disadvantage of the Soviet Union.

The stock defense of the Yalta agreement on Manchuria is that the staffs had told Roosevelt that Russia must be brought into the war in order to minimize the American casualties which would be incurred in an invasion of the Japanese homeland. But it was for the President to review this military advice in the light of the basic objectives of American foreign policy. Who was sacrificing American lives and for what end? If Stalin had demanded Alaska as his price for entering the war, most Americans would undoubtedly have considered that it would be better to have a negotiated peace with Japan than buy Russian entry into the war at such a cost.

The surrender of China's sovereign rights was not so different a case, for the United States had in fact got involved in war with Japan precisely because of a policy of opposition to Japanese domination over China, and it was a contradiction of this policy to promote a new domination over China in order to destroy the old one. When Stalin had stated his terms, the question which should have been considered was whether it was possible to have a satisfactory peace with Japan without bringing in Russia at all. In February 1945 Japan was already in fact even more thoroughly defeated than Germany, for the Japanese empire depended entirely on sea communications, and Japanese sea-power had been irretrievably smashed by the battle of the Leyte Gulf in October 1944. According to the testimony of General Bonner Fellers, General MacArthur had already before the Yalta Conference communicated to Roosevelt unofficial Japanese peace overtures amounting to acceptance of unconditional surrender but for the reservation that the Japanese monarchy should be preserved (as in the end it was).

If Japan early in 1945 had been encouraged to get out of the war in the way Italy had been, the Japanese would have had to hand over Manchuria, together with other occupied territories in China, directly to the Chinese National Government; Russia would then have had no pretext for invading Manchuria (unless Moscow were to launch an open war of aggression against China), the Chinese Communists would not have been allowed to enter Manchuria and take over the arms stocks of the Japanese army, and it is unlikely that China would be today a Communist country.

The main source of the tragedy of Yalta was an obsession in Roosevelt's mind with the idea of Big Three unity, combined with an increasing disregard of the rights of weaker nations. The Roosevelt of Yalta was no longer the man who had drafted the Atlantic Charter. During the last two years of his life he fell more and more under the spell of his vision of a world governed arbitrarily for its good by a conclave of three men. In this trend of his thinking there was probably a subtle intoxication of personal power, for the international stage enabled him to gratify that latent appetite for autocracy which he could never indulge in the domestic politics of America.

But it was necessarily Russia, and not the Western Powers, that gained by Big Three dictatorship, for it implied principles of an authoritarian, and not of a democratic, order. The democracies can never play the totalitarian game unless they themselves become totalitarian; their interest as democracies lies in a world of independent and freely associated nations, large and small. American and British policies over the last few years indicate that this lesson has made an impression. But it cannot be learned too thoroughly.

# William Henry Chamberlin:

# THE MUNICH CALLED YALTA

THE second conference of the Big Three, held at Yalta in February 1945, represented the high point of Soviet diplomatic success and correspondingly the low point of American appeasement. This conference took place under circumstances which were very disadvantageous to the western powers.

Roosevelt's mental and physical condition had disquieted Stimson at the time when the Morgenthau Plan was being approved. It certainly did not improve as a result of the strenuous presidential campaign and the long trip to the Crimean resort.

There has been no authoritative uninhibited analysis of the state of the President's health during the war. But there is a good deal of reliable testimony of serious deterioration, especially during the last year of Mr. Roosevelt's life. And it was during this year that decisions of the most vital moral and political importance had to be taken.

Among the symptoms of the President's bad health were liability to severe debilitating colds, extreme haggardness of appearance, occasional blackouts of memory, and loss of capacity for mental concentration. An extremely high authority who may not be identified described Roosevelt's condition at three of the principal conferences as follows:

"The President looked physically tired at Casablanca; but his mind worked well. At Teheran there were signs of loss of memory. At Yalta he could neither think consecutively nor express himself coherently. . . ."

It is certainly no exaggeration to say that Roosevelt was physically and mentally far less fit than Churchill and Stalin during the period when American military power was at its height and the supreme decisions which confronted the national leaders in the last phase of the war had to be taken. Had Roosevelt been able to delegate power and had there been a strong and capable Secretary of State, some of the unfortunate consequences of the President's incapacitation might have been averted and softened.

But Roosevelt clung to power with hands that were too weak to use it effectively. After his death it required much searching of files and ransacking of the memories of the participants to reconstruct what had occurred and to find out just what the President had or had not agreed to.

When Hull laid down his office on account of bad health in November 1944, his successor was Edward Stettinius. The ignorance and naïveté of the latter in foreign affairs soon became a byword to his associates in government service and to foreign diplomats. Stettinius was much better qualified to be master of ceremonies at the high jinks of some fraternal organization than to direct American foreign policy at a critical period.

Stettinius shared Roosevelt's harmful

delusion that successful diplomacy was largely a matter of establishing friendly personal contacts. At the Dumbarton Oaks Conference which shaped the preliminary draft of the United Nations charter Stettinius made himself ridiculous by cheerfully shouting "Hi, Alex" and "Hiya, Andrei" at his partners in the negotiations, the correct and pained Sir Alexander Cadogan and the sullen and bored Andrei Gromyko.

The appointment of Stettinius was due to the influence of Hopkins. The latter's star as court favorite, after a temporary eclipse, was again in the ascendant at the time of the Yalta Conference. Hopkins was a very sick man and had to spend most of his time at Yalta in bed.

Roosevelt went to Yalta with no prepared agenda and no clearly defined purpose, except to get along with Stalin at any price. He had been provided with a very complete file of studies and recommendations, drawn up by the State Department, before he boarded the heavy cruiser *Quincy,* which took him to Malta, where there was a break in the journey to the Crimea. But these were never looked at. The President suffered from a cold and from sinus trouble and his appearance "disturbed" James F. Byrnes, who accompanied him on this trip.

The conference at Yalta lasted a week, from February 4 until February 11, 1945. The principal subjects discussed were Poland, German boundaries and reparations, the occupation régime for Germany, the conditions of Soviet participation in the war against Japan, procedure and voting rights in the future United Nations organization.

At the price of a few promises which were soon to prove worthless in practice, Stalin got what he wanted in Poland: a frontier that assigned to the Soviet Union almost half of Poland's prewar territory

and the abandonment by America and Great Britain of the Polish government-in-exile in London. Roosevelt made a feeble plea that Lwów and the adjacent oil fields be included in Poland. Churchill appealed to Stalin's sense of generosity. Neither achieved any success. . . .

The protocol on reparations mentioned "the use of labor" as a possible source of reparations. Roosevelt observed that "the United States cannot take man power as the Soviet Republic can." This gave implied American sanction to the large-scale exploitation of German war prisoners as slave labor in Britain and France, as well as in Russia, after the end of the war. The Morgenthau Plan, which Roosevelt and Churchill had approved at Quebec, recommended "forced German labor outside Germany" as a form of reparations.

Procedure in the United Nations was discussed at some length. The records show that Roosevelt and Churchill were as unwilling as Stalin to forego the right of veto in serious disputes, where the use of armed force was under discussion. There was a dispute, not settled at Yalta, as to whether the right of veto should apply to discussion of controversial matters. The Russians insisted that it should, the western representatives contended that it should not. Stalin conceded this minor point when Harry Hopkins visited Moscow in June 1945.

The Soviet Government received Roosevelt's consent to its proposal that Byelorussia and the Ukraine, two of the affiliated Soviet Republics, should be granted individual votes in the United Nations Assembly. When Byrnes learned of this he raised vigorous objection, reminding Roosevelt that some of the opposition to America's entrance into the League of Nations was based on the argument that Britain would have five votes, one for each member of the Commonwealth. Roosevelt then asked for and obtained Stalin's consent to an arrangement which would give the United States three votes in the Assembly. This compensation was never pressed for and did not go into effect.

In reason and logic there was no case for giving separate votes to the Ukraine and Byelorussia. If the Soviet Union was a loose federation of independent states, like the British Commonwealth, each of its sixteen constituent republics should have been entitled to a vote. If it was a centralized unitary state, it should have received only one vote. No one with an elementary knowledge of Soviet political realities could doubt that the Soviet Union belongs in the second category. It would cause no special shock or surprise to see Canada, South Africa, Australia, or India voting in opposition to Britain on some issues. It would be unthinkable for the Ukraine or Byelorussia to oppose the Soviet Union.

So far as the Assembly is concerned, Moscow's three votes have thus far been of little practical importance. The Assembly possesses little power and the Soviet satellites are in the minority. But, as Byrnes was to discover later during the arduous negotiation of the peace treaties with Italy, Hungary, Bulgaria, Rumania, and Finland, it was an advantage for the Soviet Union to start with three of the twenty-one votes of the participating nations in its pocket.

Contempt for the rights of smaller and weaker nations was conspicuous in the Soviet attitude at Yalta. At the first dinner Vishinsky declared that the Soviet Union would never agree to the right of the small nations to judge the acts of the great powers. Charles E. Bohlen, American State Department expert on Russia, replied that the American people were not likely to approve of any denial of the

small nations' right. Vishinsky's comment was that the American people should "learn to obey their leaders."

Churchill, discussing the same subject with Stalin, quoted the proverb: "The eagle should permit the small birds to sing and not care wherefore they sang." Stalin's low opinion of France, as a country that had been knocked out early in the war, was reflected in his remark: "I cannot forget that in this war France opened the gates to the enemy."

What Stalin did forget, and what no one reminded him of, was that while France was fighting the Germans, the Soviet Government was enthusiastically collaborating with the Nazi dictatorship, sending messages of congratulation after every new victory of the Wehrmacht. French Communists, acting under Stalin's orders, certainly contributed more than other Frenchmen to "opening the gates to the enemy."

Stalin was only willing to grant France a zone of occupation on condition that this should be carved out of territory assigned to the United States and Great Britain. For a time he held out against giving France a place on the Allied Control Council for Germany. In the end he yielded to Roosevelt on this point. The President's attitude toward General de Gaulle had always been strained and chilly. But, in Hopkins's words, "Winston and Anthony [Eden] fought like tigers" for France. They enlisted the aid of Hopkins, who persuaded Roosevelt to use his influence, in this case successfully, with Stalin. . . .

Another country was offered up as a sacrifice on the altar of appeasement at Yalta. This was China. Stalin had told Hull at Moscow and Roosevelt at Teheran that he would be on the side of the United States and Great Britain against Japan after the end of the war with

Germany. At Yalta, with German military collapse clearly impending, the Soviet dictator set a price for his intervention in the Far East. The price was stiff. And it included items which it was not morally justifiable for the United States to accept. . . .

The Kurile Islands, a long chain of barren, volcanic islands extending into the North Pacific northeast of Japan proper, were to be handed over to the Soviet Union. The *status quo* was to be preserved in Outer Mongolia, a huge, sparsely populated, arid region which the Soviet Union took over without formal annexation in 1924.

South Sakhalin (which had belonged to Russia until 1905) and the Kurile Islands might be regarded as war booty, to be taken from Japan. And China had no prospect of upsetting *de facto* Soviet rule of Outer Mongolia by its own strength. But the concessions which Roosevelt and Churchill made to Stalin in Manchuria were of fateful importance for China's independence and territorial integrity.

Manchuria, because of its natural wealth in coal, iron, soya beans, and other resources, and because of the large investment of Japanese capital and technical skill, intensified after 1931, was the most industrially developed part of China. To give a strong foreign power control over its railways, a predominant interest in its chief port, Dairen, and a naval base at Port Arthur was to sign away China's sovereignty in Manchuria.

And this was done not only without consulting China but without informing China. The Chinese Government was prevented from even discussing Soviet claims in the future. For, at Stalin's insistence, the agreement to satisfy his annexationist claims was put in writing and contained this decisive assurance:

"The Heads of the three Great Powers have agreed that these claims of the Soviet Union shall be unquestioningly fulfilled after Japan has been defeated."

In the opinion of former Ambassador William C. Bullitt "no more unnecessary, disgraceful and potentially disastrous document has ever been signed by a President of the United States."

Severe as this judgment sounds, it has been borne out by the course of subsequent events. The Soviet intervention in the Far Eastern war was of no military benefit to the United States, because it took place only a few days before Japan surrendered. Politically this intervention was an unmitigated disaster.

During the Soviet occupation of Manchuria industrial equipment of an estimated value of two billion dollars was looted and carried off to Russia. This delayed for a long time any prospect of Chinese industrial self-sufficiency. As soon as Soviet troops occupied Manchuria, Chinese Communist forces, as if by a mysterious signal, began to converge on that area.

The Soviet military commanders shrewdly avoided direct, ostentatious cooperation with the Communists. After all, the Soviet Government had signed a treaty of friendship and alliance with the Nationalist Government of China on August 14, 1945. One clause of this treaty prescribed that "the Soviet Government is ready to render China moral support and assistance with military equipment and other material resources, this support and assistance to be given fully to the National Government as the central government of China."

This treaty was to prove about as valuable to the co-signatory as the nonaggression pacts which the Soviet Government concluded with Poland, Finland, Latvia, Lithuania, and Estonia. There is no indication that the Soviet Government gave the slightest "moral" or material support to the Chinese Nationalist Government. But Manchuria became an arsenal for the Chinese Communists, who were able to equip themselves with Japanese arms, obligingly stacked up for them by the Soviet occupation forces.

Soviet control of Dairen was used to block the use of this important port by Nationalist troops. Manchuria became the base from which the Chinese Communists could launch a campaign that led to the overrunning of almost all China.

Roosevelt's concessions at Yalta represented an abandonment of the historic policy of the United States in the Far East. This policy was in favor of the "open door," of equal commercial opportunity for all foreign nations, together with respect for Chinese independence. The American State Department had always been opposed to the "closed door" methods of Imperial Russia.

But at Yalta the "open door" was abandoned in a document that repeatedly referred to "the pre-eminent interests of the Soviet Union" in Manchuria. Those interests have now become pre-eminent in China. And the surrender of Manchuria to Stalin is not the least of the reasons for this development.

The Yalta concessions were a violation of the American pledge at Cairo that Manchuria should be restored to China. If New York State had been occupied by an enemy and was then handed back to the United States on condition that another alien power should have joint control of its railway systems, a predominant voice in the Port of New York Authority, and the right to maintain a naval base on Staten Island, most Americans would not feel that American sovereignty had been respected.

Whether considered from the standpoint of consistency with professed war aims or from the standpoint of serving American national interests, the record of Yalta is profoundly depressing. The large-scale alienation of Polish territory to the Soviet Union, of German territory to Poland, constituted an obvious and flagrant violation of the self-determination clauses of the Atlantic Charter. An offensive note of hypocrisy was added by inserting into the Yalta communiqué repeated professions of adherence to the Atlantic Charter.

The hopes of tens of millions of East Europeans for national independence and personal liberty were betrayed. The leaders of the Axis could scarcely have surpassed the cynicism of Roosevelt and Churchill in throwing over allies like Poland and China. The unwarranted concessions to Stalin in the Far East opened a Pandora's box of troubles for the United States, the end of which has not yet been seen.

There was not one positive, worthwhile contribution to European revival and stability in the sordid deals of Yalta, only imperialist power politics at its worst. The vindictive peace settlement, far worse than that of Versailles, which was being prepared promised little for European reconstruction. Roosevelt not long before had piously declared that "the German people are not going to be enslaved, because the United Nations do not traffic in human slavery." But at Yalta he sanctioned the use of the slave labor of German war prisoners, a throwback to one of the most barbarous practices of antiquity.

The agreements, published and secret, concluded at Yalta are defended mainly on two grounds. It is contended that military necessity forced the President to comply with Stalin's demands in Eastern

Europe and East Asia. It is also argued that the source of difficulties in postwar Europe is to be found, not in the Yalta agreements, but in the Soviet failure to abide by these agreements.

Neither of these justifications stands up under serious examination. America in February 1945 was close to the peak of its military power. The atomic bomb still lay a few months in the future. But the United States possessed the most powerful navy in the world, the greatest aircraft production in quantity and quality, an army that, with its British and other allies, had swept the Germans from North Africa, France, Belgium, and much of Italy.

The lumbering Soviet offensive in the East was dependent in no small degree on lend-lease American trucks and communication equipment. There was, therefore, no good reason for approaching Stalin with an inferiority complex or for consenting to a Polish settlement which sacrificed the friends of the West in that country and paved the way for the establishment of a Soviet puppet régime.

No doubt Stalin could have imposed such a régime by force. Only the Red Army in February 1945 was in a position to occupy Poland. How much better the outlook would have been if Churchill's repeated prodding for action in the Balkans had been heeded, if the Polish Army of General Anders, battle-hardened in Italy, had been able to reach Poland ahead of the Red Army!

But there would have been a great difference between a Soviet stooge régime set up by the naked force of the Red Army and one strengthened by the acquiescence and endorsement of the western powers. The former would have enjoyed no shred of moral authority. As it was, nationalist guerrilla resistance to the made-in-Moscow government was

prolonged and embittered. Many thousands of lives were lost on both sides before the satellite régime, with a good deal of Russian military and police aid, clamped down its rule more or less effectively over the entire country. How much stronger this resistance would have been if the United States and Great Britain had continued to recognize the government-in-exile and insisted on adequate guarantees of free and fair elections!

There was equally little reason to give in to Stalin's Far Eastern demands. The desire to draw the Soviet Union into this war was fatuous, from the standpoint of America's interest in a truly independent China. Apparently Roosevelt was the victim of some extremely bad intelligence work. He was given to understand that the Kwantung Army, the Japanese occupation force in Manchuria, was a formidable fighting machine, which might be used to resist the American invasion of the Japanese home islands which was planned for the autumn.

But the Kwantung Army offered no serious resistance to the Soviet invasion in August. It had evidently been heavily depleted in numbers and lowered in fighting quality.

Apologists for the Yalta concessions maintain that Japan in February 1945 presented the aspect of a formidable, unbeaten enemy. Therefore, so the argument runs, Roosevelt was justified in paying a price for Soviet intervention, in the interest of ending the war quickly and saving American lives.

But Japanese resistance to American air and naval attacks on its own coasts was already negligible. American warships were able to cruise along the shores of Japan, bombarding at will. According to an account later published by Arthur Krock, of the *New York Times*, an Air

Force general presented a report at Yalta pointing to the complete undermining of the Japanese capacity to resist. But the mistaken and misleading view that Japan still possessed powerful military and naval force prevailed.

Acceptance of this view by Roosevelt was especially unwarranted because two days before he left for Yalta Roosevelt received from General MacArthur a forty-page message outlining five unofficial Japanese peace overtures which amounted to an acceptance of unconditional surrender, with the sole reservation that the Emperor should be preserved. The other terms offered by the Japanese, who were responsible men, in touch with Emperor Hirohito, may be summarized as follows:

1. Complete surrender of all Japanese forces.

2. Surrender of all arms and munitions.

3. Occupation of the Japanese homeland and island possessions by Allied troops under American direction.

4. Japanese relinquishment of Manchuria, Korea, and Formosa, as well as all territory seized during the war.

5. Regulation of Japanese industry to halt present and future production of implements of war.

6. Turning over of any Japanese the United States might designate as war criminals.

7. Immediate release of all prisoners of war and internees in Japan and areas under Japanese control.

MacArthur recommended negotiations on the basis of the Japanese overtures. But Roosevelt brushed off this suggestion with the remark: "MacArthur is our greatest general and our poorest politician."

That the President, after receiving such a clear indication that Japan was on the verge of military collapse, should have

felt it necessary to bribe Stalin into entering the Far Eastern war must surely be reckoned a major error of judgment, most charitably explained by Roosevelt's failing mental and physical powers.[1]

Captain Ellis M. Zacharias, Navy expert on Japan whose broadcasts in fluent Japanese hastened the surrender, asserts that intelligence reports indicating Japanese impending willingness to surrender were available at the time of the Yalta Conference.

One such report, communicated in the utmost secrecy to an American intelligence officer in a neutral capital, predicted the resignation of General Koiso as Premier in favor of the pacific Admiral Suzuki. The Admiral, in turn, according to the report, would turn over power to the Imperial Prince Higashi Kuni, who would possess sufficient authority and prestige, backed by a command from the Emperor, to arrange the surrender.

I am convinced that had this document, later proven to be correct in every detail, been brought to the attention of President Roosevelt and his military advisers, the war might have been viewed in a different light, both Iwo Jima and Okinawa might have been avoided, and different decisions could have been reached at Yalta.[2]

Zacharias also believes that if the Japanese had been given a precise definition of what America understood by uncondi-

[1] The story of the Japanese peace overtures is told in a dispatch from Washington by Walter Trohan, correspondent of the *Chicago Tribune* and the *Washington Times-Herald*. It appeared in these two newspapers on August 19, 1945. Previous publication had been withheld because of wartime censorship regulations. Mr. Trohan personally gave me the source of his information, a man of unimpeachable integrity, very high in the inner circle of Roosevelt's wartime advisers.

[2] Captain Ellis M. Zacharias, U.S.N., *Secret Missions* (New York: Putnam, 1946), p. 335.

tional surrender as late as June, or even at the end of July 1945, both Soviet intervention and the dropping of atomic bombs on Hiroshima and Nagasaki could have been averted.[3]

Certainly there was a hopeful alternative to the policy, so disastrous in its results, of encouraging and bribing the Soviet Union to enter the Far Eastern picture. This was to aim at a quick peace with Japan, before the Soviet armies could have been transferred from the West to the East. There is every reason to believe that such a peace was attainable, if the Japanese had been assured of the right to keep the Emperor and perhaps given some assurance that their

[3] *Ibid.*, pp. 367–68.

commercial interests in Manchuria and Korea would not be entirely wiped out.

There is little weight in the contention that the Yalta agreements, in themselves, were excellent, if the Soviet Government had only lived up to them. These agreements grossly violated the Atlantic Charter by assigning Polish territory to the Soviet Union and German territory to Poland without plebiscites. They violated the most elementary rules of humanity and civilized warfare by sanctioning slave labor as "reparations." And the whole historic basis of American foreign policy in the Far East was upset by the virtual invitation to Stalin to take over Japan's former exclusive and dominant role in Manchuria.

# *Patrick J. Hurley*: TESTIMONY ON THE MILITARY SITUATION IN THE FAR EAST

**M**Y primary purpose is to show what were the underlying principles of American foreign policy at the beginning of World War II and then to show where, when, and how our State Department surrendered them and embarked our Nation on an entirely different policy. This surrender of the principles and objectives for which we said we were fighting and the support of principles completely opposite to them is responsible for the confusion and for the costly failures in American relations. We should quit supporting ideologies abroad which if successful will destroy the American system

of liberty. We should quit the policy of appeasement and present again a positive foreign policy based upon the principles of individual liberty, self-government, regulated free enterprise, and justice. . . .

There is but one element in these proceedings to which I object, and that is secrecy. I am convinced that secret diplomacy should have no place in a government by the people. In a government by the people, the people cannot make correct conclusions if they are not given all the facts. It is immoral, as well as hurtful to the welfare of the Nation, to

From *Hearings on the Military Situation in the Far East* before the Committees on Armed Services and Foreign Relations, U. S. Senate, 82nd Congress, 1st Session, 1951, excerpted material from pages 2827–2862.

permit officials to make secret commitments and follow secret policies binding all of the people without the knowledge or consent of the people.

Military plans, strategy, and tactics belong in a different category from political policies and political commitments which bring military force into operation.

Military plans should be kept secret, but policies that cause the commitment of a nation to war should not be kept from the people affected by the commitment.

The tragic thing about secrecy surrounding international commitments and policies is the fact that everything necessary for the information of the enemy leaks, and the result is that the people of America who are being committed without their knowledge are the only people kept in ignorance of what the commitments are.

Our diplomats surrendered the territorial integrity and the political independence of China in a secret agreement at Yalta.

We surrendered in that secret agreement the objectives for which we had told the American people we were fighting. Since Yalta, our Government has failed to evolve a positive foreign policy worthy of the men who have died to uphold the principles of individual liberty, self-government, and justice.

A weak and confused foreign policy after Yalta, and in general after World War II, is the primary cause for every international problem confronting our Nation and for every casualty we have suffered in Korea.

Beginning at Yalta in February 1945 our foreign policy changed from the support of the principles of the Atlantic Charter to a policy based on concessions to communism and imperalism, and fear of Russia, rather than on confidence in America. Confidence in America is a better basis for a foreign policy than fear of communism. . . .

American diplomats surrendered the territorial integrity and the political independence of China, surrendered the principles of the Atlantic Charter, and wrote the blueprint for the Communist conquest of China in secret agreement at Yalta. . . .

We should for a moment say that before the secret agreement at Yalta was signed General MacArthur had already fought his way back to the Philippine Islands; Admiral Halsey had defeated the Japanese Navy in the South China Sea.

In January, before the secret agreement was adopted, in the following February, Admiral Halsey had sunk as many as 40 Japanese fighting craft in one day. The Japanese Air Force had been defeated and almost completely destroyed. A great part of the Japanese Army was isolated in the islands and on the mainland. Japan had neither the ships nor the air force to return the Japanese Army to the Japanese Islands.

The victorious American Navy under Admiral Nimitz was in a position to prevent the return of the Japanese Army to the Japanese Islands. The victorious American Air Force under General Kenney was in a position to complete the work of destruction that it had already commenced on the Japanese fortifications.

Yet, Secretary Acheson tells you that the American people and the American Government feared the final assault on Japan would cost more than a million American casualties.

You will note this statement by Secretary Acheson did not name any military officers or any officials of the Government who feared the final assault to conquer Japan would cost a million casualties.

If we believe this statement made by Secretary Acheson, we must also believe that the final conquest of a broken and beaten Japan would cost more in American casualties than all the battles of the Pacific, all the battles of the islands, all the battles of Burma and China, all the battles of the Atlantic, all the battles of Africa, all the battles of the Mediterranean, all the battles of Italy, all the battles of England, all the battles of France, all the battles of Holland, all the battles of Belgium, and all the battles of Germany. America had less than 1,000,000 casualties in all of those battles.

You may consult any reliable almanac and you will find that American casualties in World War II, inclusive, were less than a million casualties. Yet Secretary Acheson has been telling the people for several years that it was feared that the final assault on a broken and beaten Japan would cost more casualties than were expended in all the war put together.

The fear expressed by Secretary Acheson in my opinion did not exist, but the Secretary expressed both moral and physical fear.

We turn now from the physical to the moral. America was in a position at Yalta to speak the only language the Communists understand, the language of power. The President of the United States at Yalta was in command of the greatest land, Navy, and Air Force ever assembled on earth.

One quiet sentence to Marshal Stalin in that language could have indicated that America would require him to keep his solemn agreements. That one sentence would have prevented the con-

quest of all the Balkan States, the conquest of Poland, and the conquest of China. The sentence was not forthcoming.

On the contrary, your diplomats and mine surrendered in secret every principle for which we said we were fighting. They talk about Stalin breaking his agreements, gentlemen. He never had to break one. We cowardly surrendered to him everything that he had signed and we did it in secret. President Roosevelt was already a sick man at Yalta.

The State Department released Russia from its solemn commitments and therefore brought about the conquest of other people and other nations. The surrender of principles and objectives by the State Department at Yalta created the confusion, the crisis which confronts our Nation today. . . .

What I am saying to you gentlemen is that at the time of Yalta the United States had unquestionable power to make Russia respect her solemn agreements, but instead we surrendered them in secret. Russia did not have to break her agreements or commitments. All of them were surrendered to her by American diplomats at Yalta and subsequently.

The postwar success of Russia is not due to Russia's strength but to the weakness of American foreign policy. Mr. Acheson has been telling you that all of the principles and objectives stated in the Atlantic Charter and the territorial integrity and political independence of our ally, China, were given away in secret because our State Department was convinced that Russia would not keep her commitments and was in the position to seize all of the properties that we gave her in secret.

Rather than face this threat by Russia, American diplomats weakly surrendered the objectives to which Russia and 45 other nations had agreed. The American State Department, instead of demanding that Russia respect its commitment, secretly released her from those commitments. This weakness brought about the ruthless conquest of other people both in the east and in the west. Through the weakness of the Yalta secret agreement with Russia, we have lost 450,000,000 Chinese friends in Asia.

Now let us turn for a moment to one more feature of the Yalta secret agreement. The National Government of the Republic of China was our ally. The secret agreement gave away another's property.

None of the property that we used to appease Russia belonged to the United States. As Mr. Acheson has ably said, we paid with the property of another to save American casualties and in the fear that if we didn't pay Russia, Russia would have taken it all anyway.

Here we find a very weak defense of America's secret betrayal of China and the giving away of someone else's property to protect ourselves.

I believe that the verdict of history on the Yalta agreement will mark it as both immoral and cowardly.

Secretary Acheson, in his recent testimony, attempts to set up a defense against the charge that we betrayed our ally by saying that China really liked the fact that we betrayed it in secret at Yalta — Chinese property that we gave Russia in secret — Chinese property — and kept that agreement secret from the Chinese — that the State Department had betrayed China and that the Chinese people liked the betrayal.

That defense by Secretary Acheson is absurd. I was there at the time and I know that it is not true. . . .

SENATOR WILEY. Now, as I understand it, you were not present at Yalta.

GENERAL HURLEY. I was not.

SENATOR WILEY. It is very important, sir, that in this investigation we get the judgment of men of your years and your background — on what you understand occurred at Yalta — and your understanding or any information as to who were the prime actors in that drama which so changed the world and which so affects our present economic and political life today. I would like to get your reaction to that.

GENERAL HURLEY. In the first place, I notice that some of the commentators or newsmen yesterday reported that I said the Yalta surrender was due to the cowardice of President Roosevelt.

I remember distinctly that I said that President Roosevelt was already a very sick man at Yalta, and I did not attribute to him what transpired at Yalta.

Now on the second part of your question which has been so ably stated, for me to engage like some others do in a recitation of rumors and hearsay evidence would not only be unbecoming me, but it would be unbecoming the cause in which I am appearing, and for that reason if you will permit me, Senator, I will testify to that which I know.

I was not at Yalta. There are a number of witnesses who were at Yalta, and I couldn't testify for the minute details of what happened there.

SENATOR WILEY. Well, Hiss was at Yalta, wasn't he?

GENERAL HURLEY. Yes, sir; Hiss was at Yalta.

SENATOR WILEY. Do you suggest that we subpoena Hiss?

GENERAL HURLEY. Well, I am afraid that there is a certain provision that enables a man to be relieved from testifying against himself, and I think, I don't believe you could get Mr. Hiss to tell you the facts about Yalta. . . .

SENATOR WILEY. . . . Let me put the question this way: We have heard the testimony of the Secretary and others — testimony which was certainly in part rebutted yesterday by some of your testimony — that at Yalta it appeared to be the judgment of those present to do the thing that was in the best interest of America.

Now many of us always have better hindsight than foresight — whether we were naive, whether we were just children without the world horizons before us, or whether we were inoculated by fear due to the Communist method of impacting human minds — what was it, that, let's put it kindly, made us so inept, so incompetent to foresee around the corner of tomorrow, with the result we have got what we have now.

Now your judgment on that, without indulging in any personalities, would be valuable because you were then a world figure, are now a world figure, and with your background you know something about the things that might teach us not to be so inept or so naive in the world of today and tomorrow.

GENERAL HURLEY. I am glad to answer where you asked me what would be my judgment on what occurred at Yalta.

I believe I testified yesterday that in my opinion the surrender of principles at Yalta because of fear that Russia had the power to take the property anyway is immoral — the surrender of our ally, the betrayal of our ally, China, at Yalta, because, as Secretary Acheson said, we feared that the final assault on the islands of Japan would cost a million casualties. Now we said that when I believed that Japan was already beaten

and broken. We said that when your Commander in Chief was at the head of the greatest land, Navy, and Air Force in the world.

And I said yesterday that I believed that the surrender of principles, the letting of Stalin free from the solemn commitment that he had made, the surrender of all those commitments at Yalta — I think that in my judgment the verdict of history will be that it was both immoral and cowardly.

That was my judgment on what occurred at Yalta.

SENATOR WILEY. Well, I think that is a partial answer. But unless we can get those who were present to tell us the clash of minds, we are still in the dark as to whether or not Hiss and his kindred, as the tools of the Communists, were the ones who were shaping this thing, or whether it was based upon the facts that you say did not exist but which they thought did exist.

GENERAL HURLEY. I do; and I will be glad to discuss that.

I think that the fact that men like Hiss have been shielded — we have had a lot of secret hearings by committees; we have had a lot of a star chamber executive committees set up; commissions; proceedings in all of them have been kept secret from the public. . . .

SENATOR WILEY. Again we come back to the fundamental issue.

With President Roosevelt ill, who dominated that picture at Yalta, so that the facts, apparently as you say they were, were disregarded, and other facts were assumed as the basis for action?

Who was it that dominated that picture?

GENERAL HURLEY. That I couldn't tell you, except by mere hearsay. I wasn't there. . . .

# W. Averell Harriman: STATEMENT REGARDING OUR WARTIME RELATIONS WITH THE U.S.S.R., PARTICULARLY CONCERNING THE YALTA AGREEMENT

*To the Committees on Armed Services and Foreign Relations of the Senate:*

I AM submitting this statement for use in connection with the hearings on the Far Eastern situation. My objective is to clarify the confusion that has arisen regarding the understandings reached at Yalta by President Roosevelt and Prime Minister Churchill with Premier Stalin.

Much has been said and written about Yalta and its effect on the postwar course of events. Some people have shown a lack of understanding of our objectives in the conduct of the war and our efforts during the war to lay a foundation for a peaceful postwar world. Others appear to have profited from hindsight. Still others — for reasons best known to themselves — have distorted and perverted the facts to a point where their statements have little or no basis in reality. As a result, a myth has grown up that what President Roosevelt and Prime Minister Churchill did at Yalta has led to our postwar difficulties with the Soviet Union. This myth is without foundation in fact.

The discussion at Yalta and the understandings reached there were an integral part of our negotiations with the Soviet Union throughout the war to bring the desperate struggle to a victorious and early conclusion and to find a way in which the United States, Great Britain, and the U.S.S.R. could live together in peace. The postwar problems have resulted not from the understandings reached at Yalta but from the fact that Stalin failed to carry out those understandings and from aggressive actions by the Kremlin. . . .

The question of Soviet participation in the Pacific War was discussed in some detail at Teheran. Roosevelt proposed to Stalin the basing of American heavy bombers in the Maritime Provinces north of Vladivostok. This was deemed a necessary requirement by our Air Force in order to cover the Japanese Islands. In addition, Roosevelt suggested the possible use of Soviet ports for our naval forces and requested the immediate exchange of military intelligence concerning Japan. Stalin agreed that those matters should be studied. Shortly thereafter we established exchange of combat intelligence. The other matters continued to be the subject of discussion on my part with Stalin in Moscow during the ensuing year.

Concurrently with our negotiations for the conduct of the war, President Roosevelt sought to come to an understanding

From *Hearings on the Military Situation in the Far East* before the Committees on Armed Services and Foreign Relations, U. S. Senate, 82nd Congress, 1st Session, 1951, excerpted material from pages 3328–3342.

regarding postwar problems with the Soviet Union. It was clear that unless these problems were settled we would have difficulties once the war was ended. President Roosevelt attempted to use our relationship as allies to develop a basis on which world peace could be maintained, and to settle in advance differences which we were likely to have over the treatment of territories occupied by the Red Army.

In August 1941, before Pearl Harbor, Roosevelt and Churchill had met at sea and proclaimed the Atlantic Charter, a statement of the fundamental principles to which nations must adhere if they are to live together in peace and freedom. In January 1942, at our request, the Soviet Union subscribed to the Atlantic Charter in the Declaration by United Nations. In October 1943, a further step was taken in the Moscow Declaration, which laid the foundation for the United Nations. This declaration was signed by Molotov, Eden, and Hull, and the Chinese Ambassador in Moscow. It was only after Hull's vigorous insistence that Molotov agreed to the inclusion of the signature of the Chinese. This was in line with Roosevelt's consistent attempts to strengthen the position of the Chinese National Government and to obtain the support of that Government by the Soviet Union.

At Teheran, in addition to the military matters, President Roosevelt attempted to develop further a basis for reaching political understandings with the Soviet Union. Plans for the organization of the United Nations were discussed, and also such matters as the postwar treatment of Germany, the future of Poland, and the independence of Iran. Further negotiations about these matters took place in Moscow on frequent occasions during the ensuing year and, with

respect to the United Nations organization, at Dumbarton Oaks.

Russian objectives in the Far East were also explored at Teheran, particularly with reference to the need of the Soviet Union for the use of warm water ports. I understand that Roosevelt had talked about this latter point with Chiang Kai-shek at the Cairo Conference, and that Chiang had indicated his agreement with the idea that the Port of Dairen should be internationalized.

In my talks with Roosevelt in 1943 and 1944, he told me of his concern over the historic conflicts between the Soviet Union and China, and the need for finding a basis for the settlement of the underlying causes of these difficulties.

On Roosevelt's instructions, I discussed with Stalin on a number of occasions throughout 1944 Soviet participation in the war against Japan, the concerting of our military actions in the Pacific, including operations by American bombers from the Maritime Provinces, and the basis of an understanding between the Soviet Union and the Chinese National Government. In one of these talks, which took place in June, Stalin minimized the Chinese Communists, and stated that Chiang was the only man who could hold China together and that he should be supported.

Molotov reiterated this position when Mr. Donald M. Nelson and Major General Patrick J. Hurley stopped at Moscow in August en route to Chungking.

Although Stalin had on several occasions mentioned Soviet political objectives in the East, it was not until December 1944 that he outlined these objectives to me in detail. He said that Russia's position in the East should be generally reestablished as it existed before the Russo-Japanese War of 1905. The lower half of Sakhalin should be returned to the Russians, as well as the Kurile Islands, in order to protect Soviet outlets to the Pacific. The Russian wished again to lease the ports of Dairen and Port Arthur and to obtain a lease on those railroads in Manchuria built by the Russians under contract with the Chinese, specifically, the Chinese Eastern Railway, which was the direct line from the Trans-Siberian Railroad through to Vladivostok, and the South Manchurian Railroad making a connection to Dairen. He stated that the Soviet Union would not interfere with the sovereignty of China over Manchuria. In addition Stalin asked for the recognition of the status quo in Outer Mongolia. I pointed out to Stalin that the talks at Teheran had envisaged internationalization of the Port of Dairen, rather than a lease. Stalin replied that this could be discussed. I immediately reported Stalin's proposals to President Roosevelt, and they became the basis of the discussions at Yalta.

It was against this background, which I have briefly sketched, that President Roosevelt and Prime Minister Churchill met with Stalin at Yalta in early February 1945. The question of Roosevelt's physical condition at the time of Yalta has been the subject of considerable discussion. Unquestionably, he was not in good health and the long conferences tired him. Nevertheless, for many months he had given much thought to the matters to be discussed and, in consultation with many officials of the Government, he had blocked out definite objectives which he had clearly in mind. He came to Yalta determined to do his utmost to achieve these objectives and he carried on the negotiations to this end with his usual skill and perception.

The discussions at Yalta covered a wide range of topics, including final plans for the defeat of Hitler, the occupation and control of Germany, reparations, the United Nations Conference to meet at San Francisco on April 25th, the restoration of sovereign rights and self-government to the liberated peoples of Europe, and the establishment of a free, independent, and democratic Poland through the holding of free and unfettered elections. By the Declaration on Liberated Europe, Roosevelt and Churchill obtained the pledge of Stalin for joint action to secure the fundamental freedoms for the people in territories overrun by the Red Army. . . .

Had Stalin honored these commitments taken at Yalta, Eastern Europe would be free today and the United Nations would be a truly effective organization for world security.

The last understanding to be reached was that relating to the Far East. The crucial issue was not whether the Soviet Union would enter the Pacific War, but whether it would do so in time to be of help in the carrying out of the plans of the Joint Chiefs of Staff for an invasion of the Japanese home islands. The great danger existed that the Soviet Union would stand by until we had brought Japan to her knees at great cost in American lives, and then the Red Army could march into Manchuria and large areas of Northern China. It would then have been a simple matter for the Soviets to give expression to "popular demand" by establishing People's Republics of Manchuria and Inner Mongolia. President Roosevelt sought to reduce the general assurances which Stalin had previously given to specific undertakings for the early entry of Russia in the Pacific War, to limit Soviet expansion in the East and to gain Soviet support for the Nationalist Government of China.

It should be recalled that it was only

on the second day of the Yalta Conference that General MacArthur entered Manila. The bloody battles of Iwo Jima and Okinawa still lay ahead. It was not until more than five months later that the first and only experimental explosion of the atomic bomb was successfully concluded at Alamogordo. The military authorities estimated that it would take 18 months after the surrender of Germany to defeat Japan, and that Soviet participation would greatly reduce the heavy American casualties which could otherwise be expected. The Joint Chiefs of Staff were planning an invasion of the Japanese home islands, and were anxious for the early entry of Russia in the war to defeat the Japanese Kwantung Army in Manchuria and in order that our bombers could operate from bases in Eastern Siberia.

These plans were outlined in two memoranda which were before the President at Yalta.

In a memorandum for the President, dated 23 January 1945, the Joint Chief of Staff stated:

The Joint Chiefs of Staff have been guided by the following basic principles in working toward U.S.S.R. entry into the war against Japan:

Russia's entry at as early a date as possible consistent with her ability to engage in offensive operations is necessary to provide maximum assistance to our Pacific operations. The United States will provide maximum support possible without interfering with our main effort against Japan.

The objective of Russia's military effort against Japan in the Far East should be the defeat of the Japanese forces in Manchuria, air operations against Japan proper in collaboration with United States air forces based in Eastern Siberia, and maximum interference with Japanese sea traffic between Japan and the mainland of Asia.

In a memorandum dated 22 January 1945, the Joint Chiefs of Staff stated:

1. The agreed over-all objective in the war against Japan has been expressed as follows: To force the unconditional surrender of Japan by —

(1) Lowering Japanese ability and will to resist by establishing sea and air blockades, conducting intensive air bombardment, and destroying Japanese air and naval strength.

(2) Invading and seizing objectives in the industrial heart of Japan.

2. The United States Chiefs of Staff have adopted the following as a basis for planning the war against Japan:

The concept of operations for the main effort in the Pacific —

(a) Following the Okinawa operation to seize additional positions to intensify the blockade and air bombardment of Japan in order to create a situation favorable to:

(b) An assault on Kyushu for the purpose of further reducing Japanese capabilities by containing and destroying major enemy forces and further intensifying the blockade and air bombardment in order to establish a tactical condition favorable to:

(c) The decisive invasion of the industrial heart of Japan through the Tokyo Plain.

3. The following sequence and timing of operations have been directed by the United States Chiefs of Staff and plans prepared by theater commanders:

| Objectives | Target date |
|---|---|
| Continuation of operations in the Philippines (Luzon, Mindoro, Leyte) | ———— |
| Iwo Jima | 19 February 1945 |
| Okinawa and extension therefrom in the Ryukus | 1 April–August 1945 |

4. Until a firm date can be established when redeployment from Europe can begin, planning will be continued for an operation to seize a position in the Chusan-Ningpo area and for invasion of Kyushu-Honshu in the winter of 1945–1946.

5. Examination is being conducted of the

necessity for and cost of operations to maintain and defend a sea route to the Sea of
Okhotsk when the entry of Russia into the
war against Japan becomes imminent. Examination so far has shown that the possibility of seizing a position in the Kuriles for
that purpose during the favorable weather
period of 1945 is remote due to lack of sufficient resources. The possibility of maintaining and defending such a sea route from
bases in Kamchatka alone is being further
examined.

6. The United States Chiefs of Staff have
also directed examination and preparation of
a plan of campaign against Japan in the event
that prolongation of the European war requires postponement of the invasion of Japan
until well in 1946.

These military considerations had been
the subject of careful study by Roosevelt
for a long time and they were uppermost in his mind at Yalta. President
Roosevelt personally carried on with
Stalin the negotiations leading up to the
understanding on the Far East. I was
present at the meetings when these matters were discussed and, under President
Roosevelt's direction, I took up certain
details with Stalin and with Molotov.
Neither Secretary of State Stettinius nor
any of his advisers, except for Charles E.
Bohlen who acted as the President's interpreter, had anything to do with these
negotiations. Any suggestion to the contrary is utterly without foundation in fact.

The first conversations took place on
February 8th, at which Stalin brought
up with Roosevelt the proposals which
he had presented to me the previous
December in Moscow. Stalin contended
that these proposals should be accepted.
Roosevelt said that he believed there
would be no difficulty in regard to the
Kurile Islands and the return to Russia
of the southern half of Sakhalin. He said
that, although he could not speak for
Chiang Kai-shek, he believed that Dairen

might be made a free port under an international commission, and that the Manchurian railroads might be operated
jointly. The President and Stalin also
discussed internal conditions in China.
Stalin reiterated his recognition of the
need for a united China under Chiang
Kai-shek's leadership.

Stalin suggested that the proposals be
put in writing and be agreed to before
the conference ended.

Two days later, on February 10, Molotov took up with me the details of the
understanding to be reached. I re-empha-
sized President Roosevelt's views that the
ports should be free ports and not leased
to the Soviet Union, that the Manchurian
railroads should not be leased but jointly
operated, and that in any event the
understanding should specify that the
concurrence of Chiang Kai-shek was
required.

I reported this conversation to Roosevelt, and he instructed me to explain his
views again to Molotov, which I did.

Later on in the same day, February 10,
Roosevelt and Stalin met again. Stalin
agreed to the modification as proposed
by Roosevelt, except that he maintained
that a lease on Port Arthur would be
required, as it was to be used for a naval
base. Stalin accepted the requirement
for Chiang Kai-shek's concurrence and
said that he wanted his concurrence also
to the status quo in Outer Mongolia.
President Roosevelt and Stalin were prepared to have this done, having in mind
the need for secrecy and lack of security
in Chungking. . . .

Stalin also agreed to joint planning for
military operations in the Pacific and to
the use by the United States Army Air
Force of bases in the Maritime Provinces
at Komsomolsk and Nikolaevsk.

President Roosevelt felt that he had
achieved his principal objectives. He

had obtained the agreement of the Soviet Union to enter the war against Japan within three months after the defeat of Germany. This was the period required to move Soviet troops from the European front to Siberia. It was considered to be in good time, and conformed to the plans of the Joint Chiefs of Staff which involved the redeployment of our forces from Europe to the Pacific. Roosevelt had also obtained Stalin's pledge of support for Chiang Kai-shek and recognition of the sovereignty of the Chinese National Government over Manchuria.

In recent years several objections have been leveled at the terms of the Yalta understanding on the Far East and the circumstances under which it was concluded.

It has been asserted that the understanding was a mistake because, as it turned out, Russian participation had no influence on the defeat of Japan. To President Roosevelt at Yalta, the lives of American fighting men were at stake. He had been advised by the Joint Chiefs of Staff that the defeat of Japan would take many months after VE-day and that if the Soviet Union came in soon enough countless American lives would be saved. Furthermore, up to that time, Stalin had carried out vital military undertakings. Roosevelt, therefore, considered that a definite commitment from Stalin was of supreme importance and would be of great value.

Another criticism is that Chiang Kai-shek was not consulted before the understanding was signed and that the understanding was kept secret. The question of consulting Chiang was a difficult one. Secrecy was a military necessity. Experience had shown that whatever was known in Chungking got to the Japanese. Stalin was unwilling to risk Japanese knowledge of his plans until he had been

able to strengthen his forces in Siberia. At Roosevelt's insistence, however, the understanding specified that Chiang's concurrence was required where China's direct interests were affected and that Chiang should be notified at the appropriate time.

I am sure that Roosevelt would have much preferred to have consulted Chiang in advance, if he had thought it was feasible for him to do so. On the other hand, he had had certain general talks with Chiang on some of the points involved, and knew of Chiang's desire to come to a permanent understanding with the Soviet Union. For these reasons, and also because of the strong support that he had given Chiang in the past, Roosevelt felt that he could work things out with Chiang when the time came.

Because of the prior conversation with Stalin, Roosevelt was convinced that the requirement for Chiang's concurrence qualified the provision that the claims of the Soviet Union "shall be unquestionably fulfilled," and that Stalin so understood. Events proved that Roosevelt was correct. The Yalta understanding provided a framework for negotiations between the Soviet Union and the Chinese National Government in the summer of 1945, looking toward a settlement of the long-standing difficulties between the two countries. These negotiations, which I will discuss in greater detail later in this statement, were voluntarily negotiated between the two governments and culminated in the Sino-Soviet agreements of August 1945. In these agreements, although the Soviet Union obtained certain privileges in the railroads and the ports, it fully recognized the sovereignty of the National Government over both China and Manchuria and agreed to support that government and no other. When the Sino-Soviet agreements were made public in August they were welcomed both in China and in the United States. These agreements dispose of the claim that the concessions made at Yalta regarding Manchuria undermined Chiang Kai-shek and ultimately caused him to lose control of the mainland of China. The loss of control over the mainland by the National Government was due not to the Yalta understanding but to the fact that the Soviet Union broke the Sino-Soviet agreements and to the factors which have been discussed in detail before these Committees. . . .

With regard to comments on the words "preeminent" and "lease" in the Yalta understanding, I can personally state that neither Roosevelt nor Stalin intended that the phrase "preeminent interests" should go beyond Soviet interests in the free transit of exports to and imports from the Soviet Union. President Roosevelt had told me at Yalta that this was his interpretation and, when I took his position with Stalin in August 1945, he agreed. As to the lease on Port Arthur, Roosevelt looked upon this as an arrangement similar to privileges which the United States had negotiated with other countries for the mutual security of two friendly nations.

The problem of China and the Soviet intentions in the Far East was also discussed during Mr. Hopkins' special mission to Moscow in May 1945. During a conversation which he and I had with Stalin on May 28 I brought the matter up and Stalin reaffirmed his support of a unified and stable China which would control all of Manchuria. Stalin reiterated that the Soviet Union had no territorial claims against China and stated that he would support the open-door policy. He said he would also welcome representatives of Chiang to be with his troops when they entered Manchuria in order to facilitate the establishment there of administration by the Chinese National Government.

Soviet participation in the war against Japan was again discussed at the Potsdam Conference which took place from July 17 to August 2, 1945. It will be recalled that although the first and only atomic bomb experimental explosion had been successfully concluded on July 16, the bomb had not yet been used against Japan. During the conference, Stalin informed President Truman of peace feelers which he had received from the Japanese Government. These were of such a character as to be unacceptable.

At Potsdam, more than five months after Yalta, the Joint Chiefs of Staff were still planning an invasion of the Japanese home islands and still considered Soviet participation in the Pacific War essential. On July 24, 1945, the Combined Chiefs of Staff reported to the President and the Prime Minister that their over-all strategic concept for the prosecution of the war in the Pacific was as follows:

In cooperation with other Allies to bring about at the earliest possible date the defeat of Japan by: lowering Japanese ability and will to resist by establishing sea and air blockades, conducting intensive air bombardment, and destroying Japanese air and naval strength; invading and seizing objectives in the Japanese home islands as the main effort; conducting such operations against objectives in other than the Japanese home islands as will contribute to the main effort; establishing absolute military control of Japan; and liberating Japanese occupied territory if required.

The Combined Chiefs of Staff also stated:

The invasion of Japan and operations directly connected therewith are the supreme operations in the war against Japan; forces and resources will be allocated on the required scale to assure that invasion can be accomplished at the earliest practicable date. No other operations will be undertaken which hazard the success of, or delay, these main operations.

They went on to say that our policy should be to:

Encourage Russian entry into the war against Japan. Provide such aid to her war-making capacity as may be necessary and practicable in connection therewith.

On the basis of this over-all plan, extensive discussions were carried on with the Soviet Chiefs of Staff for the attack on Manchuria by the Soviet forces about two months prior to landings by U. S. forces on the Japanese home islands.

In the meantime the Chinese Government had been informed of the Yalta understanding. In Washington on June 9, President Truman had discussed with T. V. Soong, Premier of the Chinese National Government, the provisions of the understanding, including the promise of Stalin to conclude a treaty of friendship with the National Government of China. On June 14, President Truman saw Soong again and told him of the renewed assurances Stalin had given Hopkins and myself in Moscow to support the National Government of China under Chiang. Soong expressed his gratification. On June 15 Ambassador Hurley informed Chiang of the Yalta understanding and also communicated to him Stalin's renewal of his assurances regarding China's sovereignty in Manchuria and his support of a unified and stable China and of the open-door policy.

By this time it had been agreed that negotiations would start promptly in Moscow between China and the Soviet Union regarding the matters dealt with in the Yalta understanding. T. V. Soong arrived in Moscow at the end of June 1945. Negotiations were conducted between Stalin and Molotov, on the one hand, and Soong, on the other. They were interrupted by the Potsdam Conference, but were resumed early in August, at which time Soong was joined by Wang Shi-chieh, the Foreign Minister of the Chinese National Government.

Stalin, at the outset, made demands that went substantially beyond the Yalta understanding. While Soong was not prepared to accede to all of these demands, he made it clear to me that his Government was anxious to reach an agreement with the Soviet Union, and to this end he was prepared to make concessions which we considered went beyond the Yalta understanding.

At no time did Soong give me any indication that he felt the Yalta understanding was a handicap in his negotiations. I repeatedly urged him not to give in to Stalin's demands. At the same time, during this period, I had several talks with Stalin and Molotov in which I insisted that the Soviet position was not justified. This action I took on instructions from Washington. Also, on instructions, I informed Soong that the United States would consider that any concessions which went beyond our interpretation of the Yalta understanding, would be made because Soong believed they would be of value in obtaining Soviet support in other directions. Soong told me that he thoroughly understood and accepted the correctness of this position. The fact is that, in spite of the position I took, Soong gave in on several points in order to achieve his objectives.

Events moved swiftly during the early days of August. On August 6, the first atomic bomb dropped on Hiroshima and on August 9 another on Nagasaki. On August 8, the Soviet Union entered the war against Japan. On August 10, Japan sued for peace through the Swiss Government and on August 14 an armistice was arranged. On that day a series of agreements between the Soviet Union and China including a Treaty of Friendship and Alliance, were concluded. They were ratified by the Chinese Government on August 24, 1945, and were made public at that time. The texts of these agreements are set forth on pages 585–596 of the volume entitled "United States Relations with China" and are summarized as follows on page 117:

The Treaty pledged mutual respect for their respective sovereignties and mutual noninterference in their respective internal affairs. In the exchange of notes the Soviet Union promised to give moral support and military aid entirely to the "National Government as the central government of China" and recognized Chinese sovereignty in Manchuria; and China agreed to recognize the independence of Outer Mongolia if a plebiscite after the defeat of Japan confirmed that that was the desire of the Outer Mongolian people. The agreement on Dairen committed China to declare Dairen a free port "open to the commerce and shipping of all nations" and provided for Chinese administration of the port; but it exceeded Yalta by granting the Soviet Union a lease of half of the port facilities free of charge. This agreement has not been put into effect, since Nationalist military and civil officials have been prevented from functioning in the Kwantung Peninsula area because of the attitude of the Russians and the Chinese Communists. The agreement on Port Arthur provided for the joint use of the area as a naval base by the two Powers and extended the boundary of that area farther than the United States expected, though not to the pre-1904 boundary which the U.S.S.R. would have preferred. The railway agreement provided for joint ownership and operation of the Chinese Eastern and South Manchurian Railways. The Treaty and the agreements regarding Dairen, Port Arthur, and the railroads were to run for thirty years.

Of prime importance is Article V of the Treaty of Friendship which reads as follows:

The High Contracting Parties, having regard to the interests of the security and economic development of each of them, agree to work together in close and friendly collaboration after the coming of peace and to act according to the principles of mutual respect for their sovereignty and territorial integrity and of noninterference in the internal affairs of the other contracting party.

Supplementing this provision an exchange of notes between Molotov and Wang specified:

In accordance with the spirit of the aforementioned Treaty, and in order to put into effect its aims and purposes, the Government of the U.S.S.R. agrees to render to China moral support and aid in military supplies and other material resources, such support and aid to be *entirely given to the National Government as the central government of China.*

Soong told me in Moscow he was gratified at the results obtained and expressed his gratitude for the active support the United States had given him in his negotiations. Ambassador Hurley informed the Secretary of State on August 16 from Chungking that Chiang Kai-shek was "generally satisfied with the treaty." Ambassador Hurley went on to state that at his suggestion, Chiang had invited Mao Tse-tung, Chairman of the Chinese Communist party to a conference in Chungking. His cable concluded by stating that "Chiang Kai-shek will now have an opportunity to show realistic and generous leadership." On September 6, Ambassador Hurley cabled the Department of State that: "The publication of these documents has demonstrated conclusively that the Soviet Government supports the National Government of China and also that the two governments are in agreement regarding Manchuria."

The Sino-Soviet agreements were welcomed by the American press. As a sample I quote below portions of an editorial which appeared in Life magazine on September 10, 1945:

Twelve days after Japan gave up, there was announced in Moscow and Chungking an agreement which was as great a victory for common sense as the defeat of Japan was for armed might. The Soong-Stalin treaties contain less ammunition for pessimists than any diplomatic event of the last 20 years. The signature of two men have done as much to assure peace as all our Flying Fortresses.

*     *     *

Two strong and subtle men, both revolutionaries since youth, sat down in Moscow and discovered that each needed and wanted a long peace to complete his particular revolution. So they negotiated out every major issue between Russia and China.

*     *     *

In Chungking, Mao and Chiang are now laying the basis for that (China's) future. It is extremely bright.

Certainly Americans have cause to call it bright. For the present prospects of China and a vindication of American policy in Asia for almost 50 years.

*     *     *

Peace, lively but genuine peace, is therefore the outlook.

Nothing that was done at Yalta contributed to the loss of control over China by Chiang Kai-shek. The Yalta under-standing was implemented by the Sino-Soviet agreements, which had they been carried out by Stalin, might have saved the Chinese National Government. The inability of the Chinese National Government to maintain control over China was due to the fact that the Sino-Soviet agreements were not honored by Stalin, and to other factors which have been dealt with before these Committees in great detail.

I do not believe that it would serve a useful purpose for me to discuss the subsequent course of events in China, as they have been testified to at length in these hearings by others who had direct contact with these matters.

In conclusion, I want to reemphasize the objectives that President Roosevelt and Prime Minister Churchill sought to achieve in their relations with the Soviet Union during the war.

Their primary objective was to maintain Russia as an effective fighting ally. This problem in itself gave grave concern, not only as to the military capabilities of the Soviet forces, but also as to whether the Kremlin would make separate arrangements with Hitler and leave the Western Allies stranded. The building of mutual confidence in the conduct of the war was not an easy task. But the fact remains that Russia was an effective fighting ally, and carried out vital military undertakings against Hitler.

In addition, Roosevelt and Churchill sought to lay a foundation during the war for cooperation to maintain world peace by all nations, including the Soviet Union, and to find solutions to specific problems which would result from the war, particularly with regard to the treatment of those countries which would be occupied by the Red Army. No one was under any illusions about the difficulties that we would encounter. Nevertheless, step by step, Soviet leaders subscribed to principles which culminated in the formation of the United Nations. They entered into agreements designed to dispose of many specific problems. The carrying out of these commitments would have gone a long way toward achieving Roosevelt's objective of a peaceful world. The postwar difficulties stem from the fact that Stalin did not carry out his commitments and from the fact that the Soviet Union has failed to live up to the Charter of the United Nations.

Some people claim that we "sold out" to the Soviet Union at Yalta. If this were true, it is difficult to understand why the Soviet Union has gone to such lengths to violate the Yalta understandings. The fact is that these violations have been the basis of our protests against Soviet actions since the end of the war. There would have been a sell-out if Roosevelt and Churchill had failed to bend every effort to come to an understanding with the Soviet Union and had permitted the Red Army to occupy vast areas, without attempting to protect the interests of people in those areas.

Only by keeping our military forces in being after Germany and Japan surrendered could we have attempted to compel the Soviet Union to withdraw from the territory which it controlled and to live up to its commitments. The people of the United States and the war-weary people of Europe were in no mood to support such an undertaking. This country certainly erred in its rapid demobilization in 1945, but this is an error for which the entire American people must share the responsibility. I cannot believe that anyone seriously thinks that the move to bring the boys home could have been stopped. I still recall my grave concern when I was in Moscow at the cold reception the Congress gave to

President Truman's recommendation for universal military training in the fall of 1945.

The most difficult question to answer is why Stalin took so many commitments which he subsequently failed to honor. There can be no clear answer to this question. I believe that the Kremlin had two approaches to their postwar policies, and in my many talks with Stalin I felt that he himself was of two minds. One approach emphasized reconstruction and development of Russia, and the other external expansion.

On the one hand, they were discussing possible understandings with us which would lead to peaceful relations and result in increased trade and loans from the west for the reconstruction of the terrible devastation left in the wake of the war. If they had carried out this program, they would have had to soft-pedal for the time at least the Communist designs for world domination — much along the lines of the policies they had pursued between the two wars.

On the other hand, we had constant difficulties with them throughout the war and they treated us with great suspicion. Moreover, there were indications that they would take advantage of the Red Army occupation of neighboring countries to be in a position to seize control in the postwar turmoil.

The Kremlin chose the second course. It is my belief that Stalin was influenced by the hostile attitude of the peoples of Eastern Europe toward the Red Army, and that he recognized that governments established by free elections would not be "friendly" to the Soviet Union. In addition, I believe he became increasingly aware of the great opportunities for Soviet expansion in the postwar economic chaos. After our rapid demobilization, I do not think that he conceived that the United States would take the firm stand against Soviet aggression that we have taken in the past five years.

The one great thing accomplished by our constant efforts during and since the war to reach a settlement with the Soviet Union is that we have firmly established our moral position before the world. Had these efforts not been made, many people of the free world would still be wondering whether we and not the Kremlin were to blame for the tensions that have developed. The fact that the Soviet Union did not live up to its undertakings made clear the duplicity and the aggressive designs of the Kremlin. This fact has provided the rallying point for the free world in their collective effort to build their defenses and to unite against aggression.

## *Chester Wilmot*: STALIN'S GREATEST VICTORY

IT was not altogether fortuitous that the Yalta Conference coincided with the Red Army's spectacular victory in Poland, for the timing was determined by Stalin. The original initiative had come from Roosevelt, who had been eager to arrange a meeting of the Big Three at the first opportunity after his re-election as President. On his behalf, therefore, Hopkins had broached the subject with the Soviet Ambassador in Washington, Andrei Gromyko, early in November. When Gromyko had replied that Stalin could not leave the Soviet Union, since he was personally directing the military campaign, Hopkins had suggested that the conference might be held in the Crimea. Gromyko had passed this suggestion on, but no positive response had been forthcoming from Moscow. . . .

There is no reason to believe that Stalin had anticipated Hitler's offensive in the West and had therefore delayed his reply to Roosevelt until the moment of greatest Allied embarrassment. On the other hand, the history of wartime and post-war diplomacy has made it clear that the Russians regard international conferences as opportunities for the recognition of situations which have already been created by the exercise of power, not as occasions for the negotiation of reasonable settlements mutually acceptable. Since he was more concerned with Power than Justice, Stalin was not interested in having another conference with the Western leaders until he had secured for himself the strongest military position his armies seemed capable of gaining. . . .

. . . The commitment of Hitler's entire strategic reserve in the West ensured the success of the Red Army's January offensive in Poland. Accordingly, when he cabled Roosevelt just before Christmas, Stalin had good reason to believe that by the start of the Yalta Conference he would be in possession of Warsaw and at least the greater part of Western Poland. Nevertheless, he proceeded to strengthen his position by a political

From *The Struggle for Europe* by Chester Wilmot. Copyright, 1952, by Chester Wilmot. Reprinted by permission of Harper & Brothers.

manoeuvre designed to present his Allies with a *fait accompli*. On December 30th Roosevelt and Churchill confirmed their willingness to come to Yalta early in February. On the following day, at the instigation of the Kremlin, the Lublin Committee proclaimed itself the "Provisional Government of Liberated Democratic Poland" and in the first week of the new year the Soviet Union extended to this puppet administration the diplomatic recognition it had refused to accord the legitimate Polish Government in London.

Even Stalin, however, can hardly have expected that the turn of events would swing the balance of power so quickly or so far in his favour. In the last fortnight of January, while the Russians were sweeping through Poland and into the Reich, driving before them a rabble of armies, the Americans in the Ardennes were meeting resistance as stubborn and as skillful as any they had encountered since D-day. On January 16th the converging attacks of the First and Third U. S. Armies had met at Houffalize, but no substantial body of German troops had been cut off in the Western Ardennes, and the Wehrmacht had continued to fight a steady rearguard action back to the Siegfried defences. It was February before the Americans regained the line they had been holding six weeks earlier.

On February 4th the Americans captured the first of the Roer dams towards which they had been attacking when the Germans began their counter-offensive. The forces of the Western Powers were now ready to launch their long-delayed assault on the Rhineland, but they were no nearer Berlin than they had been in September 1944, or for that matter in September 1939. Except in the Roer River sector, the Siegfried Line was still

intact; the Rhine had yet to be forced; and, since Eisenhower's engineers then believed that no large-scale crossing of the Lower Rhine could be carried out before May, there seemed little chance of Berlin being taken by attack from the West.

On the Eastern Front by this time Malinovsky, having thwarted the German attempts to relieve Budapest, was 80 miles from Vienna; Konev, having surrounded Breslau and secured several bridgeheads west of the Oder, was 120 miles from Prague; and Zhukov, having reached the Oder at Kuestrin north of Frankfurt, was 45 miles from Berlin. Thus the Soviet armies stood, with all the capitals of Eastern Europe already in their hands and the three great capitals of Central Europe within their grasp.

At Yalta Stalin was to be in a doubly advantageous position, for the conference took place not only on the morrow of a severe Allied reverse and at the moment of the Red Army's greatest victory, but also at a time of Anglo-American suspicion and discord.

En route to the Crimea, Roosevelt and Churchill held a brief preliminary conference at Malta, where they discussed the Yalta agenda and those issues which had introduced a certain acrimony into their relationship since their last meeting at Quebec in September. From these discussions Churchill hoped that there would emerge a common policy which he and the President could then present to Stalin and by their unity offset the advantage of his strength. It was apparent, however, that Roosevelt was as anxious as ever to avoid making commitments or giving the Russians any reason to think that they were dealing with an Anglo-American alliance. He saw himself as "the Good Neighbour of the World," the independent arbiter whose task it was to preserve harmony between Churchill and Stalin and to prevent Anglo-Soviet rivalry from causing a breach in "Big Three Unity." In the course of the Malta meeting the British delegation were dismayed to find that their American colleagues were less suspicious of Russia's post-war intentions than they were of Britain's. The appreciation of this fact — astonishing though it may seem at this distance — is essential to the understanding of what happened at Yalta.

The roots of this suspicion lay deep in history. Ever since 1776 Americans have nurtured a profound prejudice against "colonialism," and have tended to presume that the independence which brought them such benefits must likewise transform the lives of peoples less fortunate than themselves. With little regard for the merits, or the difficulties, of particular cases, they have consistently favoured the early grant of self-government to all dependent peoples, and particularly to those still under the dominion of the British Crown, for to Americans — by virtue of their past — Britain has remained the symbol of all Imperialism. Although ready to concede that British colonial policies were more progressive and more humane than those of any other country, they persisted in the belief that Imperial rule contained such inherent evils that even good empires must be bad. . . .

Roosevelt's "assault" upon the colonial concept began with the Atlantic Charter. The first draft of this declaration was drawn up by Churchill, who endeavoured to set forth the principles which should guide the democratic nations in their struggle against German aggression and in the re-establishment of European peace. Reporting to the House of Commons on September 9th, 1941, the Prime Minister said: "At the Atlantic meeting we had in mind the restoration of the sovereignty . . . of the states . . . now under the Nazi yoke." This, he insisted, was "quite a separate problem from the progressive evolution of self-governing institutions in the regions and peoples that owe allegiance to the British Crown."

The President, on the other hand, had no such limited view. During the Atlantic Charter Conference he told Churchill: "I can't believe that we can fight a war against fascist slavery, and at the same time not work to free people all over the world from a backward colonial policy. . . . The peace cannot include any continued despotism. Equality of peoples involves the utmost freedom of competitive trade." Thus, when he added to Churchill's draft the statement that he and the Prime Minister wished to "see sovereign rights and self-government restored to those who have been forcibly deprived of them," Roosevelt was thinking not only of the occupied countries of Europe but also of colonial peoples throughout the world. Furthermore, when he inserted an article declaring that they would endeavour "without discrimination to further the enjoyment by all states, great or small, victor or vanquished, of access, on equal terms, to the trade and to the raw materials of the world," the President was avowedly aiming at the Ottawa Agreements, the foundation of Imperial Preference. Appreciating this, Churchill demanded that the words "without discrimination" should be replaced by the phrase "with due respect to their existing obligations," but this gained him only a brief respite from American pressure.

Five months later, when the master Lend-Lease Agreement was signed, Roosevelt insisted that, in return for

American aid, Britain must agree to "the elimination of all forms of discriminatory treatment in international commerce and the reduction of tariffs and trade barriers" after the war. Cordell Hull, the prime advocate of this clause, reports that "a few Tory members of the British Cabinet . . . regarded the Lend-Lease Agreement . . . as an attempt to infringe on British Imperial sovereignty"— which, of course, it was.

In his Memoirs Hull is quite frank about the President's purpose. "We had," he writes, "definite ideas with respect to the future of the British Colonial Empire, on which we differed with the British. It might be said that the future of that Empire was no business of ours; but we felt that unless dependent peoples were assisted toward ultimate self-government and were given it . . . they would provide kernels of conflict." Neither Hull nor Roosevelt were content with the official British explanation that "self-government should be achieved within the British Commonwealth." On one occasion the President told his son, Elliott, "I've tried to make it clear to Winston — and the others — that, while we're their allies and in it to victory by their side, they must never get the idea that we're in it just to help them hang on to the archaic, medieval Empire ideas . . . Great Britain signed the Atlantic Charter. I hope they realise the United States government means to make them live up to it.". . .

Roosevelt's vision of the peace included not only the ending of the colonial system, but the abandonment of what he regarded as its essential concomitants, spheres of influence and regional balances of power. He expected, as Hull told Congress, that when the United Nations organisation was established there would "no longer be any need for spheres of influence, for alliances, for balance of power, or any other of the special arrangements through which, in the unhappy past, nations strove to safeguard their security or promote their interests."

This idealistic vision was not shared by Churchill who knew from long experience of European history that nations are less likely to succumb to the temptation of aggrandisement if their ambitions are restrained by a reasonable balance of power, and that such a balance could be preserved only by alliances and other "special arrangements." Churchill was by no means anti-Russian, but as early as October 1942 he had set down the view that "it would be a measureless disaster if Russian barbarism were to overlay the culture and independence of the ancient states of Europe." After Teheran, while continuing to work for Hitler's defeat and Stalin's friendship, he had become alive to the danger that the war would leave the Soviet Union in a position of overwhelming power which could be counter-balanced only by a strong British Empire, a firm Anglo-American alliance and a United States of Europe.

The prospect of a Russian advance deep into Central and Southeastern Europe dismayed Churchill, and was one of the main reasons for his unflagging advocacy of those Balkan operations which Roosevelt and the American Chiefs of Staff so persistently vetoed.

Thwarted in his desire to forestall Russia militarily, Churchill endeavoured to restrain her by striking a political bargain direct with the Kremlin. In the early summer of 1944, before the Red Army had made any serious inroad on the Balkans, the Prime Minister proposed to Stalin (without the President's knowledge) that the "controlling interest" in Rumania and Bulgaria should be exercised by the Soviet Union, and in Greece and Yugoslavia by Britain. When news of this proposal reached Washington, the secretive British approach to Moscow was resented, and the plan was condemned by Hull on the ground that it amounted to "the division of the Balkans into spheres of influence." In reply Churchill argued that he was not proposing to carve up the Balkans, but that in the re-establishment of civil government "someone must play the hand" and that this should be done by the power responsible for military operations in each country. Roosevelt was not altogether satisfied, but he agreed to give the arrangement a three months' trial on the understanding that it would apply only to immediate problems and would not prejudice the post-war settlement. Nevertheless, the plan remained suspect in Washington, particularly as the President gave his consent to it without consulting, or even advising, his Secretary of State!

American suspicions were sharpened when Churchill, during his visit to Moscow in October 1944, "extended the arrangement still further, even reducing to percentages the relative degree of influence which Britain and Russia individually should have in specified Balkan countries." Each of the major powers placed its own interpretation on this agreement. The Russians regarded it as a formal acknowledgement of their predominant role and interest in the Danube Basin. The British saw it as the recognition of the *fait accompli* in that region and were thankful to have preserved even a small voice in the affairs of the Danubian states and to have kept Russia out of Greece. In Churchill's opinion it was not a matter of dividing the Balkans between Britain and Russia, but of preventing the Soviet Union extending its sphere of influence over the whole peninsula. The Americans, on the other hand,

considered the agreement a betrayal of the Atlantic Charter, a sinister scheme to further Britain's Imperial ambitions. In the State Department it was denounced as "Churchiavellian.". . .

It was most tragic that such suspicion and discord should have developed on the eve of Yalta, for it seems to have led Roosevelt and some of his intimates to presume that the future threat to world peace and the independence of small nations would come not from Russia or international Communism, but from the old colonial powers, and particularly Britain. This peculiar aberration can be explained only if it is remembered that at this time Roosevelt did not believe that Stalin cherished any imperialistic aspirations.

Three days before he set out for Malta and the Crimea, Roosevelt took the oath for the fourth time as President of the United States, and, in the course of his inaugural address, declared, "We have learned to be citizens of the world, members of the human community. We have learned the simple truth, as Emerson said, 'the only way to have a friend is to be one.'"

This was the creed that Roosevelt carried to Yalta. There was, in his view, no fundamental conflict of national interest between the Soviet Union and the United States; the Russian and American peoples had so much in common that they would readily co-operate in the cause of peace and freedom if only there could be a real meeting of minds between their leaders. His trust in Stalin and his faith in his own ability to win the Soviet Union's lasting cooperation were still high, although the unhappy course of Russo-Polish relations during the past year might well have given him reason to doubt both his own personal influence and Russia's post-war intentions.

Three times since Teheran, Roosevelt had made a direct approach to Stalin in the hope of inducing him to reach a reasonable agreement with the Polish Government in London; each time he had been rebuffed and Stalin had shown no inclination whatever to allow the principles of the Atlantic Charter to apply to Poland. Nevertheless, Mikolajczyk reports — and there is no reason to disbelieve him — that, when he was in Washington in June 1944, Roosevelt told him, "Stalin is a realist, and we mustn't forget, when we judge Russian actions, that the Soviet regime has had only two years of experience in international relations. But of one thing I am certain, Stalin is not an Imperialist." Roosevelt explained to Mikolajczyk that he had not been able to take a public stand on the Polish question because it was election year, but "eventually," he said, "I will act as moderator in this problem and effect a settlement." Believing, as he had said after Teheran, that Stalin was "getatable," Roosevelt felt sure that when they met again across the conference table there would be no problem they could not solve on a "man-to-man" basis.

Roosevelt was not alone in thinking that Diplomacy by Friendship would bring a sympathetic response from Stalin. The most influential of his advisers — military and political alike — were agreed, as Hull says, that they "must and could get along with the Soviet Government," and that this would be possible if they were "patient and forbearing." The idea that they could "get along with" the Russians came more easily to the American leaders than to the British, for the United States is the great melting pot and the American people have shown an unparalleled capacity for absorbing into their own society a multitude of nationalities.

Perhaps the best exposition of Roosevelt's idea is to be found in a memorandum which Hopkins wrote six months after Yalta. "We know or believe," he said, "that Russia's interests, so far as we can anticipate them, do not afford an opportunity for a major difference with us in foreign affairs. We believe we are mutually dependent upon each other for economic reasons. We find the Russians as individuals easy to deal with. The Russians undoubtedly like the American people. They like the United States. They trust the United States more than they trust any other power in the world . . . above all, they want to maintain friendly relations with us. . . . They are a tenacious, determined people who think and act just like you and I do."

Eisenhower endorsed this view of the Russian people when he wrote, "In his generous instincts, in his love of laughter, in his devotion to a comrade, and in his healthy, direct outlook on the affairs of workaday life, the ordinary Russian seems to me to bear a marked similarity to what we call an 'average American.'" Eisenhower believed too that there was a special bond between the United States and the Soviet Union, a bond that was inevitably lacking in the Anglo-American association. He felt, he says, that "in the past relations of America and Russia there was no cause to regard the future with pessimism." On the one hand, "the two peoples had maintained an unbroken friendship that dated back to the birth of the United States as an independent republic"; on the other, "both were free from the stigma of colonial empire building by force."

This remarkable statement stems straight from the Founding Fathers. It was the American way of saying that politically both peoples were free from original sin. That this was not true of either was irrelevant; it was believed, not merely by Eisenhower but also by many Americans who should have been better acquainted with their own history. This belief was implicit in Roosevelt's approach to the problems which were to be discussed at Yalta. In his eyes, Britain was an Imperial Power, bearing the "colonial stigma"; Russia was not. That assessment of his allies was a decisive factor in Roosevelt's readiness to make concessions to the Soviet Union both in Europe and Asia in order to ensure Stalin's entry into the Pacific War.

Roosevelt's intimates give two reasons for his determination to enlist the aid of Russia against Japan. His personal Chief of Staff, Admiral Leahy, says that the President was actuated by the belief that "Soviet participation in the Far East operation would insure Russia's sincere co-operation in his dream of a united, peaceful world." On the other hand, his Secretary of State, Stettinius, reports that "immense pressure was put on the President by our military leaders to bring Russia into the Far Eastern War. At this time the atomic bomb was still an unknown quantity and our setback in the Battle of the Bulge was fresh in the minds of all. We had not as yet crossed the Rhine. No one knew how long the European War would last nor how great the casualties would be." Stettinius adds that the American Chiefs of Staff had warned Roosevelt that "without Russia it might cost the United States a million casualties to conquer Japan" and that the Pacific War might not end until 1947.

The chief advocate of this view was Marshall, but Roosevelt's military advisers were by no means unanimous in the belief that it would be necessary to invade the Japanese home islands. Leahy says that at Pearl Harbour, in July 1944, both MacArthur and Nimitz (the two commanders directly concerned) had told the President that "Japan could be forced to accept our terms of surrender by the use of sea and air powers without the invasion of the Japanese homeland." Since then, at the Battle for Leyte Gulf in October, the Japanese Navy had suffered such a crushing defeat that well before Yalta Leahy considered that the war against Japan "had progressed to the point where her defeat was only a matter of time and attrition." This was also the opinion of Arnold, the Chief of the Air Staff, whose Super-Fortresses were already bombing Japan from island airfields. There was no longer any great need for air bases in the Maritime Provinces of the Soviet Union, and, after the unhappy experiment of "shuttle-bombing" in Europe, Arnold did not set much store by any facilities he might be granted in Asia. Nevertheless, the advice of Marshall and King prevailed. . . .

Roosevelt's eagerness to buy Stalin's aid in the war against Japan was principally due to his desire to save lives, but in the light of all the evidence it seems fair to say that he was also actuated by the hope that Russia's intervention would enable the United States to strike the decisive blow at Japan, and compel her surrender, before the British, French or Dutch could regain possession of their colonies. The United States would thus be able to demand that the colonies which had been liberated from the Japanese should now be liberated from the dominion of their original owners. . . .

The plenary sessions of the Yalta Conference were held at Livadia Palace overlooking the Black Sea. The ownership of this palace had changed since it was built by the Romanoffs, but the aims and ambitions of the new owners differed little from those of its former masters. The only significant difference was that the men who now sought to fulfil Russia's imperial destiny were more ruthless and more powerful.

At the opening session on Sunday, February 4th, Stalin made a gesture which was both tactful and tactical. He proposed, as he had at Teheran, that Roosevelt should take the chair, and thus once again he brought the President half-way to his side. Yet Stalin showed no early inclination to follow the chairman's lead, least of all with regard to the President's cherished plan for creating a world peace organisation based on the recognition of the sovereign rights of all nations. The first time the subject was raised, "Stalin made it quite plain," says Stettinius, "that the three Great Powers which had borne the brunt of the war should be the ones to preserve the peace." He declared, moreover, that he would "never agree to having any action of any of the Great Powers submitted to the judgment of the small powers." In reply to this argument Churchill spoke for all the Western World in saying, "The eagle should permit the small birds to sing and care not wherefore they sang." That evening, when Stettinius and Eden discussed the outlook, they agreed that "the trend . . . seemed to be more towards a three-power alliance than anything else."

Evidently sensing that the time was not opportune to pursue the question of the world peace organisation, Roosevelt, at the start of the second plenary meeting, turned the discussion to the future of Germany. . . .

As the discussion developed — both in the plenary sessions and at meetings of the Foreign Ministers — Roosevelt and Stettinius endeavoured to take an intermediate stand on these issues. The result was that three distinct viewpoints emerged. With regard to partition, Stalin wanted a definite commitment both now and in the surrender terms; Churchill wished to make no commitments either way; and Roosevelt suggested that they should mention dismemberment in the terms without binding themselves to this policy. On the matter of reparations, Stalin demanded explicit acceptance in the Protocol of the overall figure of twenty billion dollars; Churchill opposed any mention of any figure even in a secret document; and Roosevelt inclined to the view that the Russian figure might be taken as "a basis for discussion." As for the occupation of Germany, Churchill insisted that France should have a seat on the Control Commission as well as a zone; Stalin argued against both suggestions; and Roosevelt proposed that France should have a zone but no seat.

On each of these questions the President was in fundamental agreement with the Prime Minister's stand (though not with all his reasons) but in public discussion Roosevelt played the mediator. He was not interested in upholding the balance of power concept, nor was he deeply concerned with the intrinsic merits of the German problem. To him Germany was not an issue in itself, but a bargaining point in the wider issue that was uppermost in his mind — the winning of Stalin's co-operation in the international peace organisation, and in the war against Japan.

To some extent the role of arbiter was thrust upon Roosevelt when he became chairman but there is no doubt that he preferred it since he was thus able to preserve greater freedom of action and to avoid committing himself until he had heard the rival views. The results of the President's determination to act as mediator were two fold. On the one hand, the assertion of what were in reality Anglo-American views and principles

was frequently left to the British alone
— much to Churchill's annoyance; and on
the other, as one of Roosevelt's closest
advisers [Byrnes] says, "the Soviet leaders
did over-estimate the ultimate extent of
the President's generosity and his willingness to compromise on principles."

The problem of Germany's future was
still undecided when — at the third plenary session on February 6th — Roosevelt
returned to the question of post-war
peace and asked Stettinius to review the
questions which had been in dispute at
the Dumbarton Oaks Conference. There
the Americans, British, Chinese and Russians had agreed on the principles and
purposes of what was to become the
United Nations, and had decided there
should be a General Assembly, a Security
Council and various other instrumentalities. The area of agreement had ended,
however, when the Soviet Delegate,
Gromyko, had proposed that all sixteen
republics of the Soviet Union should have
seats in the Assembly (a proposal which
"left Stettinius and Cadogan breathless"),
and had demanded that in the Security
Council the Great Powers should have the
right to veto any proposals, except those
which related to points of procedure.

It has been alleged by some of Roosevelt's critics that the establishment of the
veto power in the Security Council was
a concession made by him at Yalta to
induce Stalin to join the United Nations.
This is not so. The basic principle of the
veto was never in dispute. None of the
Great Powers was prepared to submit
itself and its interests unreservedly to the
jurisdiction of an international security
organisation. All were agreed that there
must be "unqualified unanimity of the
permanent members of the Council in
all major decisions relating to the preser-
vation of peace, including all economic
and military enforcement measures." This

was inevitable. The President, haunted
by the ghost of Wilson, insisted on the
veto power because he knew that the
United States Senate would not surrender to an international body the right to
commit American forces to military action. Churchill was equally insistent on
this point because, as he said at Yalta, he
would "never consent to the fumbling
fingers of forty or fifty nations prying into
the life's existence of the British Empire."

Although both Britain and America
felt obliged to retain the right to veto
any international "police action," they
had no desire to curtail discussion or to
prevent any small power bringing a cause
of grievance to the notice of the Security
Council. At Dumbarton Oaks, however,
Gromyko had refused to accept this view
and had told Stettinius, "The Russian
position on voting in the Council will
never be departed from!" Nevertheless,
on December 5th, 1944, Roosevelt had
sent to Stalin and Churchill a compromise formula which, while recognising
the need for unanimity on matters involving the application of sanctions, provided that on questions relating to the
peaceful settlement of any dispute no
member of the Council would cast its
vote, or exercise its veto, if it were a party
to that dispute. . . .

When the Big Three met again next
afternoon . . . Molotov proceeded to say
that the Soviet Union was "happy to accept the entire American proposal" about
voting in the Security Council, and
would not press for all sixteen Soviet Republics to be members of the United
Nations. It would be satisfactory if seats
were granted to the Ukraine and White
Russia. As it had already been agreed
that Britain, the four Dominions and
India should have individual representation in the General Assembly, Churchill
could not oppose this request, and, al-

though Roosevelt did not give his consent immediately, he told Stettinius that he "did not believe there was anything preposterous about the Russian proposal." Indeed, he regarded it as a small price to pay for Soviet co-operation.

The President and the Prime Minister were delighted at this manifestation of Stalin's willingness to join the United Nations and they felt he had made substantial concessions on two vital issues about which he had previously been intractable. They had feared that Stalin was interested only in securing a Three-Power Alliance, but now Roosevelt, at any rate, believed he had persuaded Stalin not only to recognize the sovereign rights of small nations, but also to act in friendly concert with the other great Powers in maintaining peace and extending the frontiers of freedom.

This belief was confirmed when Stalin agreed that the Soviet Union would take part in the United Nations Conference to be held in San Francisco in April, and would support there the right of the United States to have three votes in the General Assembly, if the President desired to make such a claim. It seemed to Roosevelt that these concessions were an earnest of Stalin's good faith, for it could not be foreseen then that the Soviet Union would abuse the veto power, as it was to do in the years after the war, employing it to prevent discussion as well as decision and endeavouring to exercise it even on questions of procedure. That afternoon at Yalta it appeared that Anglo-American diplomacy had gained a considerable victory, and the President felt that the long and arduous journey had not been in vain.

During the brief adjournment which followed this discussion about the United Nations the prevailing opinion among the Western delegates was that the conces-

sions Stalin had made represented a decided change of heart. Considered in relation to what followed, however, these concessions appear as a tactical manoeuvre designed to make the Western delegations more receptive to the Soviet plan for Poland which Molotov put forward while the meeting still glowed with goodwill. This plan did little more than set out in formal terms the attitude Stalin had so forcibly proclaimed the day before. The only hint of any readiness to meet the Western view was contained in the statement that the present Provisional Government (i.e. the Lublin Committee) might be enlarged to include "some democratic leaders from Polish *emigre* circles." Since the Russians refused to regard even Mikolajczyk, the leader of the Peasant Party, as a "democrat," that concession meant nothing. The moral of this day's proceedings was that, while Russia was willing to join the United Nations, she was not prepared to rely on it entirely. She intended to safeguard her own security in any event by ensuring that she had subservient neighbours in Europe and a commanding position in Asia.

Stalin's Asiatic ambitions were revealed on the following afternoon during a private discussion with Roosevelt about the Soviet Union's entry into the Japanese War. This discussion was conducted on a strictly Russo-American basis and in conditions of great secrecy. The only other persons present, apart from the two interpreters, were Molotov and Averell Harriman, the American Ambassador to the Soviet Union.

At the President's request, Churchill was not there and, when the negotiations were continued on the technical level by the Chiefs of Staff, the British did not take part. Even within his own entourage Roosevelt was most uncommunicative. Stettinius, though Secretary of State, was merely notified that talks were in progress. When he asked if the State Department should not be represented, Roosevelt replied that the problem was "primarily a military matter . . . and had best remain on a purely military level." This was a specious answer, for Stalin had long since committed himself on the basic military issue; the main point to be decided at Yalta was the political price of his participation.

It was in October 1943 that Stalin had first promised to join in the war against Japan after the defeat of Germany. He had made this offer to Cordell Hull, who says that it was "entirely unsolicited . . . and had no strings attached to it." At Teheran a month later, Stalin had repeated this promise virtually as a *quid pro quo* for the Second Front and for Lend-Lease. Nevertheless, Roosevelt had then volunteered to restore Russia's rights in the Manchurian port of Dairen and to ensure her free access to warm waters. Finding that the President was a "soft touch," Stalin proceeded to make this gesture his price with the paradoxical result that Soviet demands grew as the American need for Russian assistance in the Eastern War declined. During Churchill's visit to Moscow in October 1944, the Marshal said that "the Soviet Union would take the offensive against Japan three months after Germany's defeat, provided the United States would assist in building up the necessary reserve supplies and *provided the political aspects of Russia's participation had been clarified.* During this Moscow meeting, as on five other separate occasions in 1944, Stalin gave an assurance that Russian air and naval bases in the Maritime Provinces would be made available to American forces. In December, however, this assurance was withdrawn, presuma-

bly with a view to strengthening the bargaining position of the Soviet Union at Yalta. . . .

The President's Chief of Staff (Admiral Leahy) says that, when the Russian terms were mentioned at a subsequent plenary session, there was "little discussion and no argument." It appears that Stalin blandly explained, "I only want to have returned to Russia what the Japanese have taken from my country"; and that Roosevelt replied, "That seems like a very reasonable suggestion from our ally. They only want to get back that which has been taken from them." Churchill must have listened a little incredulously to this exchange for he cannot have forgotten that Roosevelt had once said to him: "Winston . . . you have four hundred years of acquisitive instinct in your blood and you just don't understand how a country might not want to acquire land somewhere if they can get it. A new period has opened in the world's history and you will have to adjust yourself to it."

The British should have known, if the Americans did not, that Stalin's justification could not by any means cover all the Soviet claims. The Kuriles had never formally belonged to Russia. The reclaimed "rights" in Manchuria were those which in the nineteenth century had enabled Russia to exercise in this province a degree of dominion which seriously impinged upon Chinese sovereignty. These "rights" rested on no more substantial foundations than those extraterritorial privileges which the United States, Britain and other countries had given up in 1943 at Roosevelt's own instigation and in fulfilment of his pledge to restore and respect the independence of China. To accept the "status quo" in Outer Mongolia, which Moscow had been sedulously luring away from its

allegiance to Chungking, was to acknowl-
edge that the Soviet Union, not China,
should enjoy political supremacy in that
country. In short, by this agreement
Russia was to become, with Anglo-
American consent, the political heir of
Japan in Manchuria, and thereby in
North China.

No arrangement was made at Yalta
with regard to the occupation of Korea
and the post-war fate of that unhappy
country appears to have been mentioned
only incidentally. Stalin inquired
whether it was to be occupied by any
foreign troops. When Roosevelt replied
that this was not intended, Stalin, no
doubt thinking far into the future, "expressed his approval."

Upon learning the full extent of the
Soviet terms, some of Churchill's advisers were deeply concerned, for they discovered that, although Stalin had made
no further commitments whatever and
although the most important of his
claims had to be met by their ally, China,
not by Japan, the President and the
Prime Minister were required to declare
that "these claims of the Soviet Union
shall be unquestionably fulfilled after
Japan has been defeated." Moreover,
Stalin was insisting that for security reasons the Chinese Government should not
even be informed until the Soviet Union
was ready to attack. Roosevelt had undertaken to secure Chiang Kai-shek's
compliance in due course but, as Sherwood says, "if China had refused to agree
to any of the Soviet claims, presumably
the U. S. and Britain would have been
compelled to join in enforcing them."
To some of the British delegation it
seemed rather incongruous that, while
urging Churchill to hand Hong Kong
over to China as "a gesture of goodwill,"
Roosevelt was prepared to promise Stalin
substantial concessions in Manchuria,

and to do this without so much as consulting the Chinese. This point was appreciated by at least one of his staff, for
Leahy reports that he warned Roosevelt,
"Mr. President, you are going to lose out
on Hong Kong if you agree to give the
Russians half of Dairen"; and that Roosevelt replied, "Well, Bill, I can't help it."

Eden did all he could to dissuade the
Prime Minister from setting his signature to the terms agreed upon by Roosevelt and Stalin. Churchill replied that
he must sign, because he felt that "the
whole position of the British Empire in
the Far East might be at stake." The
Prime Minister had good reason to fear
that, since he had been excluded from
the negotiations about the Japanese War,
Britain might well be excluded from
future discussions about the Far East if
she did not stand by the United States
now. Like Leahy, he may also have foreseen that, if these territorial concessions
were made to Russia, Roosevelt would
not be in a strong moral position to enforce his oft-repeated "threat" to reform
the British Empire.

Of all the agreements reached at Yalta,
this is the most controversial and would
seem to be the least defensible. Yet it
does not appear that the concessions,
which Stalin obtained, were wrung from
a reluctant Roosevelt. Sherwood records
that the President had been "prepared
even before the Teheran Conference . . .
to agree to the legitimacy of most if not
all of the Soviet claims in the Far East,"
although he expresses the opinion that
"Roosevelt would not have agreed to the
final firm commitment," if he had not
been "tired and anxious to avoid further
argument." Stettinius disagrees with this
opinion and explains that "the Far Eastern agreement was carefully worked out
and was not a snap decision made at
Yalta." He endeavours to defend the

concessions by asking: "What, with the possible exception of the Kuriles, did the Soviet Union receive at Yalta which she might not have taken without any agreement?"

That question does not pose the real issue which surely was: What did the Soviet Union receive at Yalta which she could not have taken without flagrantly violating the fundamental principles of the Atlantic Charter and the United Nations to which she had subscribed? The real issue for the world and for the future was not what Stalin would or could have taken but what he was given the right to take. This agreement provided Stalin with a moral cloak for his aggressive designs in Asia, and, more important, with almost a legal title enforceable at the Peace Conference to the territories and privileges which he demanded.

The President's surrender on this question is the more remarkable because it involved the sacrifice of those very principles which he had striven to uphold throughout his dealings with Churchill and Stalin. He had always insisted that he would not make any post-war commitments which would prejudice the peace treaties; he would recognize no spheres of influence, no territorial changes except those arrived at by mutual agreement, and no transfers of colonial territory except under conditions of international trusteeship. By making this agreement about the Japanese War, however, Roosevelt weakened both his mediating influence and his bargaining position in relation to problems arising out of the German War. He was not well placed to defend the sovereignty of Poland, once he had agreed to the infringement of China's sovereignty without her consent and in breach of the promise he had given to Chiang Kai-shek at Cairo in 1943. He could not make any

effective protest against the Russians' creating a sphere of influence in the Balkans, when he had acknowledged their sphere of influence in Mongolia and Manchuria. Having departed from his principles in Asia, he could not expect to be allowed to apply them in Europe; not against a realist like Stalin. Consequently, the President was now in a less favourable position than he had been at the start of the conference. Stalin's appetite had been whetted, not satisfied.

The records kept by those who were present at Yalta give the impression that the negotiations about Russia's part in the Pacific War on the Thursday afternoon marked the turning point in the week's discussions. If this was not realised by the Western delegations at the time, it seems to have been fully appreciated by Stalin. Thereafter, having gained the concessions which were to enable him to dominate China, he proceeded to consolidate politically the strategic advantages his armies had already secured in Europe. Stalin was better able to press his demands now, for he could play upon the sense of gratitude and cooperation he had built up in the Americans, and to a lesser extent in the British, by his agreement to help in the defeat of Japan and the creation of the international security organisation. The remaining negotiations were to prove the truth of the warning which had been sent to Washington two months earlier by the Head of the American Military Mission in Moscow ( General Deane ), an astute and not unsympathetic observer of the Soviet scene. In a letter to Marshall in December Deane had written, "We never make a request or proposal to the Soviets that is not viewed with suspicion. They simply cannot understand giving without taking, and as a result even our giving is viewed with suspicion. Gratitude cannot be banked in the Soviet Union. Each transaction is complete in itself without regard to past favours."

When the discussions about Poland were continued, as they were at each session on the last four days, the Russians gained their way on almost every point. Nothing more was heard of the President's suggestion that Poland should keep the Lwow region. The Curzon Line was accepted and this fact was duly recorded in the Protocol. With regard to Poland's western frontier, however, Stalin did not press for the formal recognition of a specific line, since he realised that neither Roosevelt nor Churchill were prepared to go beyond the Oder. He readily consented to the suggestion that "the final delimitation of the western frontier should await the Peace Conference," for in the meantime that left him free to make his own arrangements about the German territory between the Oder and the Neisse.

The Russians consented to the holding of free elections and Molotov told Roosevelt that these could be held "within a month." On the other hand, he bluntly rejected the supervision proposal, arguing that this would be "an affront to the pride and sovereignty of the independent people"! Eden endeavoured to insist on this safeguard, for he feared that any unsupervised elections would be a mockery, but at the final meeting of the Foreign Ministers Stettinius announced that "the President was anxious to reach agreement and that to expedite matters he was willing to make this concession." With regard to the setting up of a new administration, the three Ministers eventually decided upon a compromise formula which read: "The Provisional Government which is now functioning in Poland should be reorganised on a broader democratic basis with the inclu-

sion of democratic leaders from Poland itself and from Poles abroad." To this end various Polish leaders from all non-Fascist parties were to be brought together in Moscow for consultations with Molotov and the British and American Ambassadors.

When this formula was adopted at the plenary session on February 10th the Western delegates, with few exceptions, believed that they had reached, as Sherwood says, "an honourable and equitable solution." They were acting in good faith and they presumed that Stalin was equally sincere, for he also set his hand to a "Declaration on Liberated Europe" which reaffirmed the principles of the Atlantic Charter. By this Declaration the three Powers bound themselves "to build . . . a world order under law, dedicated to peace, security and freedom and the general well-being of all mankind," and agreed to act in concert "in assisting the peoples liberated from the dominion of Nazi Germany and the peoples of the former Axis satellite states of Europe . . . to create democratic institutions of their own choice."

These fine phrases were to prove less important than the terms of the Polish formula, which was so loosely worded that it left the Russians ample room to manoeuvre. Roosevelt certainly entertained some doubts on this score, for he concurred when Leahy said to him, "Mr. President, this is so elastic that the Russians can stretch it all the way from Yalta to Washington without ever technically breaking it." The essential fact was that, while the British and Americans started by refusing to accord any recognition whatever to the Lublin Committee, they ended by allowing it to be described in the communique as "the present Provisional Government of Poland." Moreover, although they had originally insisted that an entirely fresh administration should be formed, they finally agreed to the words "the Provisional Government now functioning in Poland should be reorganised." The only real difference between that formula and what Stalin had initially demanded was a change in verb; "enlarged" had become "reorganised.". . .

On that final Sunday morning at Livadia Palace neither the Americans nor the British suspected that the public communique and the secret protocol, so solemnly signed and endorsed with such expressions of mutual trust and goodwill, would soon be distorted and violated by their Soviet Allies, and that this process of distortion and violation would begin before the Prime Minister and the President had been able to report to their respective legislatures on the conference at which, they both asserted, the Great Powers were "more closely united than ever before."

In the House of Commons on February 27th, the Prime Minister declared: "The impression I brought back from the Crimea .•. . is that Marshal Stalin and the Soviet leaders wish to live in honourable friendship and equality with the Western democracies. I feel also that their word is their bond. I decline absolutely to embark here on a discussion about Russian good faith." That evening in Bucharest — despite the Yalta Declaration on Liberated Europe — Molotov's deputy (Andrei Vishinsky) issued to King Michael a two-hour ultimatum, demanding the dismissal of the Rumanian Prime Minister, General Radescu, the leader of an all-party Government.

Four days later, addressing a joint session of Congress, the President said: "The Crimea Conference . . . spells — and it ought to spell — the end of the system of unilateral action, exclusive alliances, and spheres of influence, and balances of power and all the other expedients which have been tried for centuries and have always failed. . . . I am sure that — under the agreement reached at Yalta — there will be a more stable political Europe than ever before." That evening in Bucharest, without any reference whatever to the Allied Control Commission, Vishinsky issued to King Michael a second ultimatum, demanding that he should appoint as Prime Minister Petru Groza, the leader of the Rumanian Communists. . . .

In strategy, as in diplomacy, Stalin's policy was always in tune with his postwar ambitions. Once military victory was assured, Stalin was less interested in bringing about Hitler's early downfall than he was in securing for the Soviet Union a commanding position in the heart of Europe. Although the timing of his various offensives in the last nine months of the war may have been governed very largely by tactical and logistic considerations, it is surprising how clearly these offensives fitted into the strategic pattern most likely to secure his political objectives. After reaching Warsaw, he concentrated on the drive up the Danube Valley through Bucharest and Belgrade to Budapest. Having thus gained control of the Balkans, he proceeded to complete the conquest of Poland by advancing from the Vistula to the Oder and then, though Berlin lay within his grasp, he turned his main attention to the capture of Vienna. The attack on the German capital was not resumed until it was in danger of being taken by the Americans. Finally, when the Red Army was unable to break through to Prague, Stalin bluffed Eisenhower into restraining the Allied advance so that Russia could enjoy the military honour and political advantage of liberating this capital also.

When the Second World War ended, therefore, of all the major political objectives which Stalin had sought to gain in Europe — either from Hitler or from Roosevelt and Churchill — the only one which had been denied him was control of the Black Sea Straits. The failure to secure access to warm-water ports in the Mediterranean represented the thwarting of one of Russia's traditional aims, but this was more than offset by the tremendous territorial gains she had made in Central and Eastern Europe. Since August 1939 the western frontiers of her power had been advanced 600 miles to the southwest, from the Dniester to the Adriatic, and 750 miles to the west, from the Pripet Marshes to the Thuringerwald, where the border of the Soviet Zone of Occupation ran within a hundred miles of the Rhine. With Germany destroyed, Britain and France exhausted, and the United States about to retire from active participation in European affairs, Russia could afford to go her own way, disregarding both the protests of her Allies and the provisions of the Yalta Agreement and the United Nations Charter.

There may have been a time when Stalin was prepared — as both Roosevelt and Churchill thought — to co-operate with the Western Allies on a friendly basis for the maintenance of postwar peace, but the records of the various conferences make it quite plain that the Soviet leaders never placed any great trust in international pacts or organisations. In November 1940, when Ribbentrop presented the Führer's offer of a Four-Power Alliance for the division of the world, Molotov replied that "paper agreements would not suffice for the Soviet Union; rather she would have to insist on effective guarantees for her security." By "effective guarantees" Molotov meant physical possession of strategic areas related to Russia's defence. At Yalta, although Stalin never expressed himself so bluntly, the same point was implied. He agreed to join the United Nations — very much on Roosevelt's terms — but at the same time he expected to be given a free hand in what he regarded as Russia's proper sphere of influence, and especially in Poland.

In Stalin's mind this became the test of Anglo-American sincerity. Roosevelt and Churchill had both declared that they would not tolerate the establishment in Poland, or any other country on Russia's borders, of a government hostile to the Soviet Union. But they had also insisted upon "free and unfettered elections" with a secret ballot and universal suffrage. Stalin knew that these two principles were mutually exclusive, since any free election in any of the states of Eastern Europe would be certain to result in the return of a non-Communist Government suspicious of, if not openly antagonistic to, the Soviet Union. Consequently, in the months following Yalta when the American and British Governments made an issue of "free elections" in the western sense, Stalin not unnaturally concluded that their real objective all along had been to set up a *cordon sanitaire* which would curtail his sphere of influence.

When the Polish question was discussed at Yalta, Potsdam and innumerable other conferences, Stalin persistently stressed the fact that Russia must have a "friendly" Government in Warsaw and that the Poles must be strong enough to hold the corridor by which the Germans had so often invaded Russia. While it was only natural that Stalin should be concerned about the security of his country, the treatment which Poland has received at the hands of the Soviet Union since the war indicates that Stalin's real concern was not security but expansion. For him Poland was the gateway *to* the West. Unless he were to control Poland, he would not have free access to Central Europe, and he needed to dominate Central Europe, and especially the Bohemian Mountains in order to protect not the Soviet Union but her conquests in the Balkans. He was clearly determined to make certain that Russia secured for herself the fruits of victory. And why not? It was for these that she had fought. . . .

The "Unconditional Surrender" formula, though the President's brain-child, was the natural result of the American determination to wage the war to absolute victory without regard to the political consequences. Roosevelt certainly had noble and unselfish political aims — the winning of Russia's friendship and the setting up of a United Nations Organisation which would preserve peace and enforce throughout the world the principles of the Atlantic Charter. Carried away by this idealistic vision and convinced of his own ability to "handle" Stalin, Roosevelt failed to foresee that the immediate political situation arising out of the war might thwart the fulfilment of his ultimate political dream. The success of his policy really depended on his ability to maintain by personal contact over the conference table the spirit of "Big Three" co-operation which, he believed, he had established at Teheran and maintained at Yalta. But Roosevelt seems to have made no allowance for the possibility that one or more of the three leaders might be removed from the scene by death or political defeat. As it happened, he himself suffered the first of these fates and Churchill the second before the world struggle ended.

Roosevelt's death revealed the gap between his hopes and the realities of the situation, but it did not create that gap.

This had been created already by his failure — and that of his Chiefs of Staff — to take account of post-war political factors in the determination of Allied strategy. That failure, the cause of so much of Europe's present suffering, had its origin partly in the immaturity of the Americans and partly in their history. At the risk of over-simplification, it may be said that the traditional attitude of the people of the United States to the recurrent conflicts of Europe is that war as a means of national policy is morally wrong. Consequently, the United States, if driven to war in self-defence or to uphold the right, should seek no national advantage or aggrandisement. Her sole purpose should be to bring about the defeat and punishment of the aggressor. Her aim should be Victory, nothing else. Since America fights for no political objective, except peace, no political directives should be given to American commanders in the field. They should be completely free to determine their strategy on military grounds alone, and the supreme military consideration is to bring hostilities to an end. To pursue a political aim is to practise Imperialism.

This was the doctrine applied by Marshall and his colleagues in the conduct of the war against Germany, although, with an ambivalence not uncharacteristic of the American people, it was not always applied in relation to the war against Japan. In the last eighteen months of the European conflict when Churchill became increasingly alarmed about Soviet policy, he sought to persuade the Americans that the military strength of the Western Allies should be employed in a manner calculated to achieve the double purpose of defeating Germany and preventing the Soviet Union from becoming too powerful. Only in Greece and Denmark was he success-

ful, and in the former case his action provoked a public rebuke from Roosevelt's
Secretary of State. Elsewhere he was repeatedly balked by American policy
which stood on the twin pillars of Roosevelt's belief that Stalin had no aggressive
ambitions and Marshall's determination
to concentrate on victory in the field. . . .

The history of Europe reveals only too
sharply the unhappy consequences of the
policy which was pursued by the Americans and, until late in the war, by the
British as well. Writing in 1941, Liddell
Hart outlined these consequences in a
statement which reads now like a
prophecy:

If you concentrate exclusively on victory,
with no thought for the after-effect, you may
be too exhausted to profit by the peace, while
it is almost certain that the peace will be a
bad one, containing the germs of another
war. This is a lesson supported by abundant
experience. The risks become greater still in
any war that is waged by a coalition, for in
such a case a too complete victory inevitably
complicates the problem of making a just and
wise peace settlement. Where there is no
longer the counter-balance of an opposing

force to control the appetites of the victors,
there is no check on the conflict of views and
interests between the parties to the alliance.
The divergence is then apt to become so
acute as to turn the comradeship of common
danger into the hostility of mutual dissatisfaction — so that the ally of one war becomes
the enemy in the next.

The two most serious miscalculations of
the Second World War both concerned
the Soviet Union: Hitler's miscalculation
of Russia's military strength, and Roosevelt's miscalculation of Russia's political
ambition. It was these two errors of
judgment which gave Stalin the opportunity of establishing the Soviet Union
as the dominant power in Europe. It is
clear now that the Western democracies
cannot afford to make another miscalculation about Russia's military power or
political intentions. A third mistake might
well be fatal to Western civilisation. It
is equally clear that, even though Stalin
may have no intention of precipitating
another world war, there is not likely to
be any lessening of the tension in Europe
or Asia. . . .

## Edward R. Stettinius, Jr.:
# APPEASEMENT OR REALISM?

THE record of the Conference shows
clearly that the Soviet Union made
greater concessions at Yalta to the United
States and Great Britain than were made
to the Soviets. The agreements reached
among President Roosevelt, Prime Minister Churchill, and Marshal Stalin were,

on the whole, a diplomatic triumph for
the United States and Great Britain. The
real difficulties with the Soviet Union
came *after* Yalta when the agreements
were not respected.

The main Russian concessions at Yalta
were:

From *Roosevelt and the Russians* by Edward R. Stettinius, Jr. Copyright, 1949, by the Stettinius
Fund, Inc. Reprinted by permission of Harold Ober Associates.

## (1) *The World Organization.*

(a) The Soviet Union accepted the American formula for voting in the Security Council. John Foster Dulles reported to the American delegation at San Francisco on May 26, 1945, that "Ambassador Gromyko recently had told him the voting formula represented a big compromise from the Russian point of view."

It was clear in the discussions at Yalta that Marshal Stalin was primarily interested in an alliance of Great Britain, the United States, and the Soviet Union. By securing his agreement to the American voting formula, however, President Roosevelt was able to achieve more than an alliance of the Great Powers.

It is absolutely incorrect to state that the permanent members were granted the veto power on most questions only because of Russian insistence. The American delegation, at Dumbarton Oaks and after, favored the big-power veto on matters involving economic and military sanctions. The United States delegation had been advised that the Secretary of War, the Secretary of the Navy, and the Joint Chiefs of Staff were agreed, as a matter of fundamental military policy, that the United States should not join any world organization in which its forces could be used without its consent. The veto was also favored by the members of Congress who were consulted on the plans for the United Nations.

The whole controversy over the veto power of the permanent members of the Security Council overlooks the fact, anyway, that it is not the veto itself but the misuse of power to veto that has impeded the effectiveness of the Security Council.

(b) The Soviet Union withdrew its request for sixteen votes in the face of the adamant position of the United States and Great Britain. The Soviet Union withdrew its request that Great Britain and the United States agree *at Yalta* to invite the Ukraine and White Russia to the San Francisco Conference. The President and the Prime Minister did pledge to support admission of the two, when the San Francisco Conference voted on this matter. The additional votes in the Assembly were not too significant. They have not been an important factor in the work of the United Nations one way or the other. The effectiveness of the United Nations has been limited by the inability of the Soviet Union, Great Britain, and the United States to work together in an amicable fashion, not because the Soviet Union has three votes in the Assembly.

In view of the many concessions made by the Soviet Union to the American position on world organization, the two additional votes were only a minor concession to the Russians. It was far wiser, President Roosevelt decided, to meet the request of the Soviet Union on this point and to secure its participation in a United Nations conference than possibly to drive it entirely out of participation in a world organization. Whether some people like it or not, we live in an interdependent world. Although the achievement of One World is beset with immense difficulties, Russian participation in the United Nations was and is a necessary step in the right direction.

President Roosevelt expressed this point of view in his message to Congress on March 1, 1945, in the following words:

When the conclusions reached with respect to voting are made known I think and I hope that you find them fair — that you will find them a fair solution of this complicated and difficult problem — I might almost say a legislative problem. They are founded in justice, and will go far to insure international co-operation for the maintenance of peace....

This time we are not making the mistake

of waiting until the end of the war to set up the machinery of peace. . . .

The structure of world peace cannot be the work of one man, or one party, or one nation. It cannot be just an American peace, or a British peace, or a Russian, French, or a Chinese peace. It cannot be a peace of large nations — or of small nations. It must be a peace which rests on the co-operative effort of the whole world. . . .

(c) The Soviet Union agreed to the American definition of the countries that should be invited to attend the San Francisco Conference. As a result these Associated Nations who declared war by March 1, 1945, were able to participate in the conference as original members. This decision made it possible for a number of Latin-American nations, particularly, to participate in the conference. Here was a substantial concession that Stalin made at the urging of Mr. Roosevelt.

(d) President Roosevelt insisted on the right of full and frank discussions in the world organization. Although the Soviet Union did not like it too well, the President made it clear that all nations had the right to be heard. As a result, the smaller nations have been able to use the United Nations as a forum to present their views to the world.

(2) *Military Co-ordination.*

At President Roosevelt's request Marshal Stalin agreed, for the first time in the war, that there should be real co-ordination of Russian and Western military activities. Stalin also agreed with the President's request that Soviet air bases near Budapest and elsewhere be made available for use by the United States Air Corps.

There was, for the first time as well, a frank statement by the Soviet Union of its future plans for offensive operations.

(3) *The French Zone of Occupation and France's Membership on the German Control Commission.*

Very early in the Conference the Soviet Union withdrew its objection to the recommendation made by the President and the Prime Minister that the French be assigned a zone of occupation from the British and American zones.

Near the close of the Conference, when President Roosevelt announced that he now agreed with the British that the French should also be on the Control Commission, the Soviet Union withdrew also its vigorous opposition to this proposal. The German zones of occupation were worked out by the European Advisory Commission in London. The zones were drawn before Yalta. I know of no evidence to support the charge that President Roosevelt agreed at Yalta that American troops should not capture Berlin ahead of the Red Army. General Eisenhower has written that the decision that American troops should not push into Berlin was taken in March 1945, solely on military grounds.

(4) *German Reparations.*

This was one of the most controversial issues at the Conference. Both Great Britain and the United States agreed on the principle of exacting reparations from Germany but we were most anxious to avoid the disastrous experience of reparations after World War I. The British did not wish to agree to the Russian figure of twenty billion. President Roosevelt was willing that the Russian figure be considered by the Reparations Commission *on its initial studies* only as a *basis for discussion* and not as an agreed amount. The Soviet Union accepted the American position.

In July 1946, V. M. Molotov, at a meeting of the foreign ministers, stated that

President Roosevelt at Yalta had agreed to ten billion dollars of reparations for the Soviet Union. This was incorrect. The President accepted, purely *as a basis for discussion* by the Reparations Commission, the figure of twenty billion dollars, fifty per cent of which was to go to the Soviet Union. Maisky at the foreign ministers' meeting on February 10 at Yalta (and Molotov was present) agreed that the reparations formula "did not commit the Allies to the exact figure." Marshal Stalin at the plenary session that same day stated that no commitment as to figures was involved. The figures mentioned, he explained, would be used merely *as a basis for discussion* by the Reparations Commission.

(5) *The Soviet Union Accepted Two British Amendments to the Agreement on Yugoslavia.*

(6) *The "Declaration on Liberated Europe."*

The American draft was accepted with almost no opposition. When Marshal Stalin realized that President Roosevelt would not accept two amendments proposed by Molotov, the Marshal withdrew them.

(7) *Poland.*

The Polish issue proved to be the most controversial and the most difficult of all the questions considered. While President Roosevelt was meeting with Prime Minister Churchill and Marshal Stalin in the Crimea, American and British troops had just recovered ground lost by the Battle of the Bulge. The Allies had not yet bridged the Rhine. In Italy our advance had bogged down on the Apennines. The Soviet troops, on the other hand, had just swept through almost all of Poland and East Prussia, and had reached at some points the Oder River in Germany. Most of Hungary had been liberated, eastern Czechoslovakia had been captured, and the Yugoslav Partisans had recaptured Belgrade in November 1944. By February 1945, therefore, Poland and all of eastern Europe, except for most of Czechoslovakia, was all in the hands of the Red Army. *As a result of this military situation, it was not a question of what Great Britain and the United States would permit Russia to do in Poland, but what the two countries could persuade the Soviet Union to accept.*

(a) President Roosevelt refused, as did the Prime Minister, to accept the Russian request that the western boundary of Poland be the western Neisse River. Marshal Stalin finally withdrew this demand and agreed to leave the western frontier of Poland to be settled at the peace conference.

(b) The Curzon Line was insisted upon by Marshal Stalin as the eastern frontier of Poland. The Soviet Union considered that the area east of that line had been taken from it by force after World War I. Before the Yalta Conference Churchill had already supported the Curzon Line in the House of Commons.

President Roosevelt suggested that the Soviet Union might consider leaving the Polish city of Lwow and some oil lands to Poland, and the Prime Minister also suggested that some such gesture would be reassuring to the world. Stalin, however, insisted that he could not be "less Russian" than Curzon and Clemenceau, who had first agreed to this frontier line. However, he did later propose minor deviations of from six to eight kilometers in favor of Poland. The United States was in no position at Yalta to change the Russian attitude on the eastern boundary.

(c) By the time of the Yalta Conference the Soviet Union had established the Lublin Provisional Polish Government. Both President Roosevelt and Prime Minister Churchill adamantly *refused* to recognize this puppet regime. Agreement on the government of Poland proved to be the most difficult and time-consuming question at Yalta. The Soviet Union insisted that all that should be done to the Lublin Government was to *enlarge* it. President Roosevelt and the British insisted that it had to be *reorganized* so as to include democratic leaders from outside Poland.

Stalin finally agreed to the *reorganization* of the Lublin Government by the inclusion of democratic leaders from at home and abroad. He also agreed with the British and American request that free and unfettered elections would be held at an early date. Roosevelt withdrew the phrase from the American formula that "The Ambassadors of the three powers in Warsaw following such recognition would be charged with the responsibility of observing and reporting to their respective Governments on the carrying out of the pledge in regard to free and unfettered elections." Although President Roosevelt did withdraw this wording, he made it clear that the ambassadors *would nonetheless still perform this function.* The sentence was reworded, therefore, to read that the three powers ". . . will exchange Ambassadors with Poland by whose reports the respective Governments will be kept informed about the situation in Poland."

It is true, of course, that the decision was not as clear-cut as President Roosevelt had desired. President Truman, in discussing the Polish agreement with me on April 21, 1945, expressed regret that the agreement was not more clear-cut, but added that he realized President Roosevelt had made every effort to make it crystal-clear.

The agreement on Poland was, under the circumstances, a concession by Marshal Stalin to the Prime Minister and the President. It was not exactly what we wanted, but on the other hand, it was not exactly what the Soviet Union wanted. It was not a "sellout" of democratic Poland, as has been so widely charged, but a pledge from Stalin that he would allow a new government to be organized and that free elections would be held in a country which was entirely at his mercy. The trouble was not the Yalta formula but the fact that the Soviet Union later failed to live up to the terms of the agreement.

President Roosevelt told a joint session of Congress on March 1, 1945: "I am convinced that this agreement on Poland, under the circumstances, is the most hopeful agreement possible for a free, independent, and prosperous Polish State."

The President also pointed out: "The responsibility for political conditions thousands of miles away can no longer be avoided, I think, by this great nation. . . . The United States now exerts a tremendous influence in the cause of peace. . . . The United States will not always have its way 100 per cent — nor will Russia nor Great Britain. We shall not always have ideal solutions to complicated international problems, even though we are determined continuously to strive toward that ideal. But I am sure that — under the agreements reached at Yalta — there will be a more stable political Europe than ever before. . . ."

What did the Soviet Union gain in eastern Europe which she did not already have as the result of the smashing victories of the Red Army? Great Britain and the United States secured pledges at Yalta, unfortunately not honored, which did promise free elections and demo-cratic governments.

What, too, with the possible exception of the Kuriles, did the Soviet Union receive at Yalta which she might not have taken without any agreement? If there had been no agreement, the Soviet Union could have swept into North China, and the United States and the Chinese would have been in no real position to prevent it. It must never be forgotten that, while the Crimea Conference was taking place, President Roosevelt had just been told by his military advisers that the surrender of Japan might not occur until 1947, and some predicted even later. The President was told that without Russia it might cost the United States a million casualties to conquer Japan. It must be remembered too, that at the time of the Yalta Conference it was still uncertain whether the atomic bomb could be perfected and that, since the Battle of the Bulge had set us back in Europe, it was uncertain how long it might take for Germany to crack. There had been immense optimism in the autumn of 1944, as Allied troops raced through France, that the war was nearly over. Then came the Battle of the Bulge, which was more than a military reversal. It cast a deep gloom over the confident expectation that the German war would end soon. In Washington, for instance, the procurement agencies of the armed services immediately began placing new orders on the basis of a longer war in Europe than had been estimated.

With hindsight, it can be said that the widespread pessimism was unwarranted. The significant fact is not, however, this hindsight but the effect of this thinking on the strategy and agreements made in the Crimea. It was important to bring the Soviet Union into the united sphere of action. Russian co-operation in the

Japanese war ran parallel to their co-operation in the world organization and to united action in Europe. Furthermore, critics of the Far Eastern agreement have tended to overlook the fact that in the agreement the Soviet Union pledged that China was to retain "full sovereignty in Manchuria" and that the Soviet Union would conclude a pact of friendship with the Chinese Nationalist Government. It is my understanding that the American military leaders felt that the war had to be concluded as soon as possible. There was the fear that heavy casualties in Japan or the possible lack of continuous victories would have an unfortunate effect on the attitude of the American people.

President Roosevelt had great faith in his Army and Navy staffs, and he relied wholeheartedly upon them. Their insistent advice was that the Soviet Union had to be brought into the Far Eastern war soon after Germany's collapse. The President, therefore, in signing the Far Eastern agreement, acted upon the advice of his military advisers. He did not approve the agreement from any desire to appease Stalin and the Soviet Union.[1]

It is apparently the belief of some critics of the Yalta Conference that it would have been better to have made no agreements with the Soviet Union. Yet if we had made no agreements at Yalta, the

[1] Admiral Ellis M. Zacharias, formerly Deputy Chief of Naval Intelligence, has written that the Joint Chiefs of Staff persuaded President Roosevelt to make the concessions in order to bring the Soviet Union into the Japanese war on a wholly inaccurate and misleading intelligence report. There was no evidence at Yalta that any intelligence reports other than the one used were in existence. See Zacharias, "The Inside Story of Yalta," *United Nations World,* January 1949, Vol. 3, No. 1, p. 16. . . . (Editor's note: Zacharias asserts that at least two other accurate intelligence reports were available, one prepared in the War Department and one prepared by him-

Russians still would have been in full possession of the territory in Europe that President Roosevelt is alleged to have given them. The failure to agree would have been a serious blow to the morale of the Allied world, already suffering from five years of war; it would have meant the prolongation of the German and Japanese wars; it would have prevented the establishment of the United Nations; and it would probably have led to other consequences incalculable in their tragedy for the world.

President Roosevelt did not "surrender" anything significant at Yalta which it was within his power to withhold. The agreements, on the other hand, speeded up the end of the war and greatly reduced American casualties. The Yalta Conference, also, made it possible to create the United Nations. Although events since Yalta have made it difficult for the United Nations to operate effectively, I am convinced that the United Nations can still become the greatest achievement of history toward the building of a stable and peaceful world.

On March 15, 1945, after I had returned to Washington from the Chapultepec Conference at Mexico City, I told a bipartisan group of senators that "the atmosphere at Yalta was not one of bickering, that Stalin and his government apparently had made up their minds to take their place among the United Nations. During the talks, the Russians fre-

self, but that both had been pigeon-holed somewhere in the Pentagon. Neither of them reached the Joint Chiefs of Staff, who acted on the basis of an intelligence document which over-estimated enemy strength. This report, says Zacharias, was overly pessimistic due to its purely quantitative rather than qualitative evaluation of the Japanese Army. According to him, both the Joint Chiefs of Staff and the War Department intelligence section were relatively unfamiliar with the situation in the Far East, as compared, for example, to Europe.)

quently made concessions on a variety of political, economic, and security matters." When Senator Tom Connally said that there was talk that President Roosevelt had given in to Stalin on almost every issue, I emphasized that "at the end of the first day at Yalta it was apparent that we faced a reasonable situation at the Crimea Conference."

I had made a similar statement to President Vargas of Brazil, on February 17, while I was visiting him in Rio. I told Vargas that "I was gratified to be able to report that President Roosevelt had found a high degree of co-operation on the part of Stalin." I also said, "It was apparent within the first forty-eight hours that they would get along and accomplish great results." When President Vargas asked if Stalin "was a very tough man to work with," I replied that "he was very tough but he was also very realistic." I explained to President Vargas that "the President was confident that the Soviet Union had decided to take its place in the United Nations family as a good citizen. . . ."

From my close association with Franklin D. Roosevelt, I know that he was primarily motivated by the great ideal of friendly co-operation among nations. At the same time he had no illusions about the dangers and difficulties of dealing with the Soviet Union. He emphasized many times that we must keep trying with patience and determination to get the Russians to realize that it was in their own selfish interest to win the confidence of the other countries of the world. We must help them see, he said, that co-operation with other nations was the only way they or we could have a peaceful world. If the Russians could acquire confidence in a world organization, the President was convinced that much could be accomplished. Although he knew that the winning of Russian confidence in a world organization would be difficult, and would take time and patience, peace was too vital a necessity not to make a supreme effort toward achieving this goal.

It was with this in mind that President Roosevelt told Congress on March 1, 1945:

. . . For the second time, in the lives of most of us, this generation is face to face with the objective of preventing wars. To meet that objective, the nations of the world will either have a plan or they will not. The groundwork of a plan has now been furnished and has been submitted to humanity for discussion and decision.

No plan is perfect. Whatever is adopted at San Francisco will doubtless have to be amended time and again over the years, just as our own Constitution has been.

No one can say exactly how long any plan will last. Peace can endure only so long as humanity really insists upon it, and is willing to work for it, and sacrifice for it.

Twenty-five years ago, American fighting men looked to the statesmen of the world to finish the work of peace for which they fought and suffered. We failed them. We failed them then. We cannot fail them again, and expect the world to survive.

I think the Crimean Conference was a successful effort by the three leading nations to find a common ground for peace. It spells — and it ought to spell —the end of the system of unilateral action, exclusive alliances and spheres of influence, and balances of power and all the other expedients which have been tried for centuries and have always failed.

We propose to substitute for all these a universal organization in which all peace-loving nations will finally have a chance to join.

I am confident that the Congress and the American people will accept the results of this conference as the beginnings of a permanent structure of peace upon which we can begin to build, under God, that better world in which our children and grandchildren — yours and mine, and the children and grandchildren of the whole world — must live, can live. . . .

President Roosevelt was well aware of the nature of Soviet society. Its dictatorial and authoritarian aspects were as repugnant to him as to any American. But he also had a strong sense of history. He knew that no society was static, and he believed that the United States could do much, through firmness, patience, and understanding, over a period of time in dealing with the Soviet Union to influence its evolution away from dictatorship and tyranny in the direction of a free, tolerant, and peaceful society.

While this process of evolution was taking place, we could faithfully support the United Nations Charter over a span of years and use the United Nations in every possible way to keep the world on an even keel and enable it to ride out without disaster the inevitable strains and stresses of the times. This, I believe, was the essence of Roosevelt's policy toward the Soviet Union as expressed at Yalta.

It was essential that Prime Minister Churchill and President Roosevelt make an honest attempt at Yalta to work with the Russians. For the peace of the world, they had to make every effort to test the good faith of the Soviet Union. Until agreements were made and tested, the world could not clearly know of the difficulties of securing Russian compliance with agreements. The Western nations could not follow their present policy toward the Soviet Union unless they had behind them the record of President Roosevelt and Prime Minister Churchill in their joint effort to deal with the Russian leaders in an honest and honorable manner at Yalta.

# Charles E. Bohlen: TESTIMONY CONCERNING HIS NOMINATION AS AMBASSADOR TO RUSSIA

THE CHAIRMAN. What was your position at Yalta?

MR. BOHLEN. I was primarily an interpreter, but at the time of Yalta, I was an assistant to the Secretary of State and one of my duties was to serve as liaison officer with the White House.

I was appointed to that position in December 1944 by Mr. Stettinius when he became Secretary of State. At Yalta I served primarily in the capacity of an interpreter for President Roosevelt but was also an adviser to the delegation. . . .

SENATOR SMITH. In dealing with the disposition of Chinese property and Chinese issues at Yalta, Chiang Kai-shek definitely was not invited. I have heard that Mr. Stalin definitely objected to his being there because he wanted to talk with Messrs. Roosevelt and Churchill about this particular setup he was working for as the price of Russia entering the Japanese war. That probably is a true report.

MR. BOHLEN. I had never heard that Stalin had objected to an invitation to Chiang Kai-shek being present at Yalta. I had never heard that it had ever been considered because the Soviet Union and Japan were not at war, and that was the reason why, for example, the Soviet Union was not represented at Cairo. In other words, there were two wars going on; there was the war in Europe in which the Soviet Union was a belligerent, and there was the war in the Pacific in which the Soviet Union was not involved. In fact, even diplomatic relations were maintained between the two countries, and I had heard — I cannot swear to this because I was not in on all these discussions — that if they were going to deal with the war in the Far East the Russians were not prepared to join in any such conference, that is, openly and officially, discussing a far-eastern war in which they were not involved.

My only background knowledge in regard to this far-eastern matter was that once the United States made the decision that we were going to invade the Japanese mainland, a decision which I believe, was made at the second Quebec Conference in the fall of 1944, certain things automatically followed in its wake. One of these was the importance of getting the Soviet Union into the Pacific war, not as is popularly supposed at any time, but in time to do some good, so to speak, in time to save American lives.

Now, clearly the agreement on the Far East was unnecessary. The estimates which were given to the President and to Mr. Churchill prior to Yalta proved to be erroneous. Whether the intelligence was faulty, in war you cannot take chances, and the estimate given to them officially and formally by their military staffs was that the war in the Pacific would last 18 months after V-E Day.

From *Hearings on the Nomination of Charles E. Bohlen* before the Committee on Foreign Relations, U. S. Senate, 83rd Congress, 1st Session, 1953, excerpted material from pages 2–113.

In those circumstances the whole question of Russia's entry into it became a matter of considerable military importance, and the tragic thing about it was that it was unnecessary. There was no invasion of Japan; Russia's involvement was not in any sense necessary.

Another feature which, I think, no one would undertake to defend politically, as it were, was the fact that it was done behind the backs of the Chinese. My understanding then was that the reason for that was grounds of military security. If the Soviet Union was coming into the war 2 or 3 months after the end of V-E Day, obviously it would be of great advantage for Japan to know that well in advance of the events. She might have been disposed herself to make some military move involving Russia. Those were the reasons given, sir. . . .

SENATOR HICKENLOOPER. . . . Getting back to the Yalta and the Cairo agreements, it is understandable that under certain theories Mr. Stalin did not attend the Cairo Conference at Cairo because he was not at war with Japan, and at Cairo President Roosevelt and Chiang Kai-shek discussed Japanese affairs. They did not at Cairo discuss the disposition of any Russian property. But at Yalta, when Mr. Roosevelt and Mr. Churchill and Mr. Stalin talked, they did discuss the disposition of Chinese property —

MR. BOHLEN. That is true.

SENATOR HICKENLOOPER (continuing). And General Chiang was not present.

MR. BOHLEN. That is true.

SENATOR HICKENLOOPER. I mean in one case, one might excuse or one might see a reason for the absence of Stalin, because nothing affecting him particularly as to his property or claimed property was discussed. At Yalta, however, they whacked up some property that China thought basically hers.

MR. BOHLEN. It is true that Chinese representatives were not present.

SENATOR HICKENLOOPER. Yes.

It runs in my mind that evidence was disclosed that the Air Force and the Navy and a substantial number of important Army people advanced the idea at Yalta and before that Japan was practically on her knees at that time; that 75 or 80 percent of her shipping had been destroyed and it would not be actually necessary for a large-scale invasion of Japan and, therefore, not necessary for Russia to come in. Do you have any knowledge of that?

MR. BOHLEN. No, sir; I have no knowledge. But I believe that the decision reached by our military authorities was to invade the Japanese Islands; I think the date had even been tentatively fixed as November 1, 1945. The decision had been made at the second Quebec conference; that is all I know of it. . . .

I think there was the belief that Russia's entry into the war before we hit the islands would save hundreds of thousands of American casualties. Such was the opinion which, I think, was the reason and, I think, the justification or excuse — it was the reason why it was considered of such overriding importance to get the Soviet Union into the war. The disposition of Chinese territories, as you know, was subsequently embodied in the Soviet-Chinese Treaty of August 1945, which was almost universally hailed in this country, as well as, I believe, in China, as a great event, because this treaty involved the recognition by the Soviet Union of the sovereignty of the Chinese Nationalist Government over Manchuria.

Now, the fact that they did not abide by that treaty is another matter; but when it was concluded it was very widely acclaimed as a great omen for the future, and an intelligent and common-sense disposition of the problems between Russia and China.

The first reaction from the Chinese was not one that they had been sold, as it were, down the river. Mr. T. V. Soong in his negotiations in Moscow found the Yalta agreement of considerable use to him as a backstop.

There are now, in retrospect, two valid criticisms of the agreement: First it was unnecessary, the war did not take the course predicted; and, secondly, it was done without the participation of the Chinese Government, . . .

SENATOR HICKENLOOPER. To make historic facts current here, there was some evidence that Mr. Roosevelt was told before he went to Yalta — the words, I think, were 99 percent a certainty — by a colonel from the Manhattan district who was sent especially to the Mediterranean, and who got on a gunboat to tell Mr. Stettinius on the way to Yalta that the atomic bomb was a practical certainty, and that with it the Japanese could be brought completely to heel without the necessity of a large-scale invasion. But in those matters I assume you had no knowledge?

MR. BOHLEN. I had no knowledge at all of the atom bomb until the late Spring of 1945, just before the test was made, but I think in this connection, just from the point of view of the historical record, that on January 23, 1945, there was a memorandum for President Roosevelt from the Joint Chiefs of Staff which states that Russia's entry at as early a date as possible consistent with her ability to engage in offensive operations was necessary to provide maximum assistance to our Pacific operation.

SENATOR FERGUSON. What is the date of that?

MR. BOHLEN. January 23, 1945. It is quoted in Mr. Harriman's statement to the committees.

SENATOR HUMPHREY. Senator Hickenlooper, what was the first explosion in the flats?

SENATOR HICKENLOOPER. August 5 or 6, 1945.

SENATOR SPARKMAN. No. August 6 was the date it was dropped. It was exploded out here in May.

SENATOR HUMPHREY. Alamogordo was in May 1945. And, yet, a colonel, in 1944, said it was a certainty?

SENATOR HICKENLOOPER. Yes.

MR. BOHLEN. Senator, I think the date was July 16, 1945; it was at Potsdam that the notification came to President Truman of the success at Alamogordo.

SENATOR HICKENLOOPER. It was the middle of the year.

SENATOR HUMPHREY. Who was this colonel?

SENATOR HICKENLOOPER. Colonel Considine. He met Mr. Stettinius on a cruiser just outside of Malta. Mr. Stettinius was on his way from Malta to the Yalta conference. That testimony is on the record. . . .

SENATOR SPARKMAN. . . . Now, a minute ago you said that, if I understood you correctly, the Yalta decision was wrong because, first, it was not necessary to get Russia into the war. You are speaking now from hindsight rather than what was actually true at that time, are you not?

MR. BOHLEN. That is right, and I would like to make that very clear, that I do not consider that the men who made the agreement at Yalta considered that they were playing a low trick on Nationalist China. They did not look upon it in that way.

As I say, the embodiment of this agreement in a treaty was, so far as I am aware, welcomed in China. There was certainly no belief at Yalta on the part of President

Roosevelt and Mr. Hopkins that they were selling out an ally.

And, as I say, the thing turned out to be unnecessary because the military estimate of the course of the war in the Pacific was not borne out by facts. But I am convinced —

SENATOR SPARKMAN. Of course, the military estimate was naturally changed with the great success of the atomic bomb —

MR. BOHLEN. Why, certainly.

SENATOR SPARKMAN (continuing). Which had not even had its preliminary explosion.

MR. BOHLEN. That is correct.

SENATOR SPARKMAN. They did not even know the mechanism would work at the time of Yalta.

MR. BOHLEN. That is right.

SENATOR SPARKMAN. Mr. Bohlen, I was a member of the Military Affairs Committee of the House, and I remember very clearly General Marshall's discussion before our committee of affairs at the time Germany collapsed, and after Yalta, in which he was preparing us for the terrific losses which we would sustain when we invaded Japan. . . .

SENATOR FERGUSON. Mr. Bohlen, you said that you were an assistant to the Secretary of State at Yalta?

MR. BOHLEN. Yes, sir.

SENATOR FERGUSON. I note that Mr. Alger Hiss was the Deputy Director, Office of Special Political Affairs, Department of State —

MR. BOHLEN. Yes, sir.

SENATOR FERGUSON (continuing). At Yalta.

MR. BOHLEN. That is true, sir.

SENATOR FERGUSON. Would you tell us what his job entailed, what his duties were?

MR. BOHLEN. Hiss was present in the delegation at the plenary sessions of the conference but took no part in them, because no one spoke except the President, or on occasion the Secretary of State. I am absolutely certain that Hiss never saw President Roosevelt in a capacity of adviser to him and never had any interviews with him except that first one when the President met the whole delegation before the opening of the Conference.

Mr. Hiss was not present at any of these discussions on the Far East between President Roosevelt and Stalin, and was at none of the private meetings with Stalin.

SENATOR FERGUSON. Do you know whether or not he prepared any data or obtained any information upon which the agreements were had?

MR. BOHLEN. If he had, it was for Mr. Stettinius, because he was attached to the State Department delegation. I was sort of betwixt and between in that I had to be with the President for interpreting purposes.

But from what I saw of Mr. Hiss' activities at Yalta, he confined himself to problems of the United Nations, the voting formula, and to matters pertaining to the establishment of the United Nations.

SENATOR FERGUSON. You have indicated that you believed that the Yalta agreement was not necessary, so far as the Far East was concerned.

MR. BOHLEN. What I meant, sir, was — what Senator Sparkman is quite right about — were the advantages of hindsight, and I might almost add the advantages of hindmyopia, because the terrific compulsions of the war are absent when you look at it 10 years afterward. The agreement at Yalta on the Far East was, as I understood it, based upon the military estimate that we were going to have to invade the Japanese Islands, which would involve very large American casualties, and that Russia's entry into the war before the landing would result in the elimination or containment, in its proper military sense, of the Kwantung Army.

SENATOR FERGUSON. Yes.

MR. BOHLEN. I say it was unnecessary, because the military development did not turn out as foreseen, but I think that in the course of a war the men who were responsible for its conduct cannot afford to underestimate the enemy, and there is a healthy and natural tendency to overestimate him because to underestimate is to court catastrophe.

SENATOR FERGUSON. The other criticism, if it was a criticism, was that Chiang Kai-shek or anyone connected with the Chinese Government was not present.

MR. BOHLEN. Yes, sir. I think that, in general, it is distasteful, to put it mildly, to do things involving another country without the representative of that country present; but there the major considerations were secrecy and security. . . .

SENATOR FERGUSON. Was not this agreement in relation to the Far East, as far as it gave other peoples' rights and liberties and lands away, in violation of the Atlantic Charter?

MR. BOHLEN. I think I have answered that in saying, Senator, that the Yalta agreement in itself was not a final definitive international instrument. The definite instrument was the treaty between China and the Soviet Union of August 1945.

SENATOR FERGUSON. Yes; but we are talking about the agreement, whether it was morally right or wrong, or whether it was just a misinterpretation of the agreement that was wrong; what I want to know is whether or not the giving of this land of another power, another nation, was not in violation of the Atlantic Charter?

Did we not say there that there would be no aggrandizement? Was it not a violation of that?

MR. BOHLEN. I do not consider that the Yalta agreement, in effect, did that.

SENATOR FERGUSON. What did it do? It agreed that we would use our influence.

MR. BOHLEN. That we would support that position.

SENATOR FERGUSON. We would support that position, which was in violation of the Atlantic Charter, was it not?

MR. BOHLEN. Well, sir, I do not think that the Atlantic Charter was against any territorial adjustments between countries. Perhaps my understanding of it is erroneous. . . .

SENATOR FERGUSON. Do you know how we agreed to, as is indicated by Sherwood on Roosevelt and Hopkins when he states:

The conclusions from the foregoing are obvious: Since Russia is the decisive factor in the war she must be given every assistance, and every effort must be made to obtain her friendship. Likewise, since without question she will dominate Europe on the defeat of the Axis, it is even more essential to develop and maintain the most friendly relations with Russia.

Did you ever hear of that before?

MR. BOHLEN. No sir; I never had until I read it in the book. I have no idea who prepared that memorandum. I think there is something in the book that says it was prepared by a military adviser for Quebec or something of that nature.

SENATOR FERGUSON. Do you know whether or not that was the basis of the agreements at Yalta and Teheran?

MR. BOHLEN. Nothing that I saw would support it that that was the basis.

SENATOR FERGUSON. Well, looking at the agreements, do you not think that is exactly what they were doing? Were they not treating Russia as being the dominant figure after the war, and were not these concessions being made to her for the purpose of allowing her to become the dominant figure?

MR. BOHLEN. No, sir; I would not say that that was the general purpose as I saw it. I think that it is, perhaps, necessary for me here to give a little background, which requires an act of memory and some imagination to put yourself back into the circumstances of the greatest war that has ever been fought.

At the time of Yalta, the Russian armies were in virtually full occupation of Poland; they were very close to the German border; offensives which had been undertaken in the latter part of January or the middle of January had brought them almost up to the German Silesian border, and there was only a small part of northeast Poland that was not under Soviet occupation.

I think the Soviet armies were very near Vienna, and were well across Hungary at the time of Yalta.

I think most of the agreements relating to Europe, therefore, were agreements which, in effect, dealt with areas which were under Soviet control, and I would like to say here that in all my experience at these conferences, the Russians were most reluctant to discuss any of the problems of Eastern Europe. They clearly would have preferred no agreement whatsoever in regard to Poland and those matters. They had physical possession by that time of Poland through their armies. They had installed their own government, which grew out of the so-called Lublin Committee in Poland, and I know that those of us who worked on Poland — and I did, myself — felt that we were trying to do everything we could to lay down some ground rules for developments in these countries and if they had been lived up to, sir, I think Eastern

Europe would not now be in the enslaved condition that we find it.

SENATOR FERGUSON. Did that not bring you to the conclusion that any agreements that you made would be interpreted so as to give her absolute control of Europe, as it was indicated in the Quebec agreement that we knew that she was going to be the dominant power, and we were playing to give her the dominant power?

MR. BOHLEN. I would not from what I saw, Senator, agree with that statement. I do not know who prepared that document that is quoted in the book, but it is the first time I had ever heard of it or seen it.

SENATOR FERGUSON. Is it part of the State Department —

MR. BOHLEN. Not that I know of, sir. I think that the map of Europe, as we look at it today, and what we call the Iron Curtain is the line roughly where the armies of the Soviet Union and the armies of the western allies met, which were set by the zonal limits. . . .

SENATOR FERGUSON. Well, wouldn't you say that the Yalta agreement, the Teheran agreement, is now the basis of the situation in Europe?

MR. BOHLEN. No sir; I would not.

SENATOR FERGUSON. Both East and West?

MR. BOHLEN. I would not.

SENATOR FERGUSON. You would not?

MR. BOHLEN. I would not, sir. I believe that the map of Europe would look very much the same if there had never been the Yalta Conference at all.

SENATOR FERGUSON. You don't say then that these agreements are the cause of this enslavement?

MR. BOHLEN. I don't, sir. I say it is the violation of them.

SENATOR FERGUSON. That is what I say.

MR. BOHLEN. What I am saying, sir, I

think in this business just because a policy failed doesn't mean it was a wrong one. In other words, I don't think the men who backed the League of Nations were necessarily wrong, despite the fact that the League of Nations failed to prevent World War II. . . .

THE CHAIRMAN. Senator Ferguson, you mentioned Hiss. Is the record clear as to what part he played, if any, according to this witness?

MR. BOHLEN. As I said earlier this morning, Hiss at that time was in charge of the section of the Department of State dealing with the United Nations. As far as I personally know, he dealt with that at Yalta and confined his activities to that.

He may have done some other things for Secretary Stettinius at the Foreign Ministers' meeting, at which I was not present. I can testify under any form of oath necessary that he was not present at any of these meetings between Stalin and President Roosevelt, and as far as I am aware, he knew nothing whatsoever about this far eastern matter.

THE CHAIRMAN. Will the Senator yield? I want to get the record clear there.

Do I understand that according to your recollection, while you acted as interpreter for President Roosevelt, between Stalin, Molotov, and Roosevelt, at no time was Hiss present?

MR. BOHLEN. He was not present, sir, at any of these private meetings. Hiss would be present when you had the large plenary sessions of the conference, at which maybe 10 or 15 or more people from the United States delegation were present.

As I explained this morning, I think possibly an explanation of the way the conference was organized might be helpful. At 4 o'clock in the afternoon the top three would meet, the President, Mr.

Churchill, and Stalin, with their advisers, with their Foreign Ministers, and then the people sitting in the back row with the other members of the delegation.

In the mornings the Foreign Ministers would meet, and I did not attend those meetings as a regular thing. Then occasionally — I think there were three such meetings during the Yalta Conference — the President alone with Stalin. When I say alone, I mean without Mr. Churchill.

At those meetings there were the President and Mr. Harriman, and Stalin, Molotov, and the two interpreters. I have no recollection or no record of the President's meetings with Mr. Churchill, which occurred somewhat more frequently I would say; nor of any of Mr. Churchill's private meetings with Stalin, so I can testify that at these private meetings between the President and Stalin, Alger Hiss was not present.

SENATOR KNOWLAND. Mr. Chairman, at that point will the Senator yield?

SENATOR FERGUSON. Yes; I yield.

SENATOR KNOWLAND. Pardon this interruption. I have here the book by Stettinius called *Roosevelt and the Russians: The Yalta Conference*, and on page 83 he says:

This Saturday night dinner was the last leisurely social gathering at the Yalta Conference. The pressure of the next few days was most exhausting. My usual daily schedule, for instance, was to confer with Matthews, Bohlen, and Hiss, just after I got up in the morning. I next discussed the conference problems with the President.

That is on page 83. Then a little farther down on page 83 he says:

After these dinners, I usually conferred with Matthews, Bohlen, Hiss, and Foote, read cables from the Acting Secretary of State through to Washington, drafted cables to the Department, and then went to bed.

Then on page 84, Secretary Stettinius says:

The next morning at 10:30, Harriman, Matthews, Hiss, Bohlen, and I met with the President on the sun porch overlooking the sea to review our proposals for the conference agenda. We arrived just before the President's meeting with the military chiefs broke up. Since the military chiefs were about to leave, I suggested that they remain in order that they might be fully informed of the diplomatic position of the State Department, and thus be in a position to correlate this with the secret military conferences that were to take place within the Chiefs of Staff of the three countries.

Now there are other references to Mr. Hiss, but that at least to me would seem to indicate that he did more than merely sit in on these large plenary meetings.

MR. BOHLEN. I thought the question was whether Hiss had been present at these private meetings between President Roosevelt and Stalin.

SENATOR KNOWLAND. As I understood Senator Ferguson, what he was trying to get at was what kind of a part did Mr. Hiss play at these Yalta conferences.

Now, we recognize, as you have testified, and I think all the books on the subject rather indicate, that the actual discussions with Mr. Stalin and Mr. Churchill were carried on either by the President or, in rare instances, perhaps by Mr. Stettinius, but what we are trying to find out, I assume from the line of questioning, is what influence, if any, Mr. Hiss may have played which he could have done either at preliminary meetings or at other gatherings that were outside of the plenary sessions.

MR. BOHLEN. What Mr. Stettinius is talking about is meetings that are always held in conferences of that kind. Hiss was there as an adviser to the Secretary

of State, not there as an adviser to President Roosevelt direct, and at these meetings my recollection is that Hiss' part in it dealt virtually exclusively with the United Nations business, which was, of course, a very big subject. . . .

[1]THE CHAIRMAN. I would like to ask one question. With respect to what Senator Knowland read from Mr. Stettinus' book about Stettinius starting the day by consulting with you and Hiss at the Yalta Conference, I think it would be very interesting if you could tell us what the subjects were that you talked about.

MR. BOHLEN. Senator, since that has been read, I have been trying to rack my memory to figure out exactly what we did discuss and whether these meetings actually took place every morning.

Insofar as my memory serves me, they were more or less means to find out where we stood, what had happened the day before, and for the orderly conduct of business to take place.

What had been referred to the Foreign Ministers from the previous day's meeting, what was expected of them, what they were to report on for the forthcoming day, I would say my recollection is they were almost exclusively procedural, rather than policy decisions. As I say, with respect to most of these agreements, with the exception of the far-eastern one, the United States policy had been well established before we went to Yalta. There were some changes that occurred in negotiations.

THE CHAIRMAN. What part of the discussion did Hiss take part in?

MR. BOHLEN. As I say, I can't recall Hiss expressing an opinion on anything about Poland, the Far East, or anything. I do recall his expressing his opinion

---

[1] NOTE: A portion of page 58 is included here out of place so as to put it in topical order.

about the United Nations matters. But I wouldn't trust my memory to the extent of saying he never did.

But, by and large, my picture of what happened is that when the subject of discussion came around to — let's say the voting formula in the United Nations, that he was the man who spoke to that. That was his particular job at this conference.

SENATOR FERGUSON. But he heard what was going on.

MR. BOHLEN. Oh, yes; he heard what was going on. . . .

SENATOR FERGUSON. Well, as it turned out now, it (Yalta Agreement) has had a great influence on what has happened in China.

MR. BOHLEN. I think that is a matter of opinion, Senator.

SENATOR FERGUSON. You don't think so?

MR. BOHLEN. I don't think it did; no, sir.

SENATOR FERGUSON. You don't think it had anything to do with what happened in China?

MR. BOHLEN. Well, everything has something to do with something, but I don't believe that it was the cause of what subsequently happened in China insofar as this treaty between the Chinese and the Soviets went, in its intended effect.

I say "intended effect" advisedly; that on the whole I think that that was a help to Chiang Kai-shek rather than a hindrance in the major business of establishing his sovereignty over China.

Now, that is a matter of opinion, and I am just giving you mine.

SENATOR FERGUSON. Did Russia agree to do anything in this agreement other than to come into the war?

MR. BOHLEN. Well, recognition of Chiang Kai-shek's sovereignty over Manchuria was the important element em-bodied in the treaty. I have not the text of the treaty here, but I think it says that the Soviet Government recognizes as the sole supreme authority in Manchuria the Nationalist Chinese Government, and that the representatives of that Government should be permitted to go up into that area even while the Soviet armies are in occupation.

SENATOR FERGUSON. Now, didn't this agreement in regard to Japan make the course easier for the Soviet Union in northeast Asia, especially in Manchuria and Korea, after the defeat of Japan, and thus facilitate the Communist conquest of China, and after that the Communist armed invasion of South Korea?

MR. BOHLEN. These are purely matters of opinion, Senator.

SENATOR FERGUSON. What is your opinion on it?

MR. BOHLEN. My opinion is that they did not, in this sense. I am not a Far East expert. I have no firsthand knowledge of China. I have not been engaged in that end of the business.

In this testimony, I don't want to divest myself of the slightest responsibility that I have for these matters. On the other hand, in the interest of accuracy, I don't think that I should take on responsibilities that were not mine. So, when I give you an opinion on this point, it is an opinion of a non-expert in oriental matters.

I think the Communist conquest of China is one thing, and the terms of the treaty another. . . .

SENATOR FERGUSON. Now, do you know that after the Teheran Conference the Polish general headquarters became aware of the fact that military responsibility over Poland had been shifted to Soviet Russia? . . .

MR. BOHLEN. With regard to the question of the relief for dropping supplies to the Warsaw garrison in August 1944, we had a considerable row with the Russians over that. Mr. Harriman was Ambassador, and he had several knockdown, drag-out fights and finally they allowed one flight to go in and drop the supplies. Some flights were made there and back —

SENATOR FERGUSON. Wasn't that before Yalta?

MR. BOHLEN. Yes, sir; it was.

SENATOR FERGUSON. And, therefore, shouldn't we have understood that Russia was dominating the situation in Poland and intended to do so?

MR. BOHLEN. Yes; their armies were in Poland.

SENATOR FERGUSON. And then why would we make an agreement providing for free elections when we knew that they wouldn't carry out free elections, and that their idea of free elections was no elections at all really?

MR. BOHLEN. Do you consider, Senator, if I might, myself, ask a question, that it would have been better to have made no agreement about Poland?

SENATOR FERGUSON. It would have been better to make an agreement whereby we would have had something to say about the elections.

MR. BOHLEN. How would you do that, Senator?

SENATOR FERGUSON. Then why did you make any when you knew the Russians wouldn't carry them out?

MR. BOHLEN. I don't think that you knew for certain.

SENATOR FERGUSON. Why did we have to surrender the rights of these people and be a party to the surrender?

MR. BOHLEN. I don't consider that the agreement of Yalta involved a surrender. It involved the opposite.

Whether or not the Russians carried out, sir, is to my mind a very different question. I think the agreement on that part of the Polish agreement is about the best you could put down on paper as to what you hoped the Russians would do and they put their signature to.

The fact that they violated it I don't think means that the agreement was bad.

SENATOR FERGUSON. Then you wouldn't have been a party to an agreement that you knew or should have known was not going to be carried out.

MR. BOHLEN. I think this is an important problem.

If agreements made as written are all right and provide for the things that this country believes in, such as free elections, universal suffrage, if you have doubts as to whether the other party is going to carry them out, it still seems to me that it is worthwhile to set your opinion of what ought to happen, and if you are able to get the other fellow to agree to it, I think in the parlance of diplomacy, that that is what it is all about.

SENATOR FERGUSON. In other words, you would favor a settlement in Korea, even when anticipating that it wouldn't be carried out. In other words you want to get an agreement that would look good on paper.

MR. BOHLEN. No, sir; I don't think that is the point.

SENATOR FERGUSON. Isn't that what happened in these agreements?

MR. BOHLEN. No, sir. The point is that you were confronted at Yalta on the question of Poland which had been the subject of intense correspondence over a period of years between the Soviet, American, and British Governments. . . .

. . . The problem you were faced with at Yalta was what were you really going to do about Poland. There were three courses of action that were open.

1. You could have, by just accepting the total *fait accompli*, let it go and do nothing about it, which is what I think

Stalin would have preferred by all indications.

2. To stick completely with the London government in exile, which would have meant that no member of it would have been in Poland. There wouldn't have been any entry into Poland on the part of anybody.

3. To attempt to get as many members of the Polish group in London as possible into the reorganized government.

Yes, but the other alternative was this. You had the country, Poland, which the Russians were in occupation of. The alternatives were leaving, washing your hands, so to speak, of the whole business, and leaving this complete Communist government, which would be worse.

The other alternative of just sticking with the London government amounted to almost the same thing, because you would have had an exile government in London and you would have had nothing in Poland, and they would have had nothing. . . .

SENATOR FERGUSON. And Poland was not present at these divisions.

MR. BOHLEN. That is true, but it was not possible to have Polish representatives present.

SENATOR FERGUSON. Well, no one representing Poland was present. It was just like the case of Chiang Kai-shek. No one representing China was present.

MR. BOHLEN. Well, the question is what do you do about a situation, Senator? And I think nothing would be easier if you had to do them all over again, you would probably do them with greater perfection, although in many ways under the compulsions of the times I don't know what you would have done that would have a great improvement over this. I will say this. I think more care could have been used in all of these agreements

as to how they looked, that is to say, from the point of view of the record. I don't know if you were thinking of what you could do to assist Poland, which I can assure you was the major motivation in the minds as I saw it of the President and Winston Churchill — they had no other interests than that; they felt very strongly on this subject.

I think the tragic fact is that by the progress of the war, which short of some drastic revision of strategy, the map of Europe as we see it today was almost made by the war itself. I think very few people have any illusions.

SENATOR FERGUSON. We were making political agreements of division prior to the ending of the war.

MR. BOHLEN. It is true in this sense.

SENATOR FERGUSON. And we did it without consultation with our own allies who were fighting in the war.

MR. BOHLEN. I think the President felt, and so did Mr. Churchill, that they were in effect trying to fight the battles for the Poles which the Poles were not able to do themselves.

Now I don't know whether these judgments were mistaken, whether there were better ways to do it, but I am utterly and totally convinced that that was the main thought. That the British had very strong feelings about Poland, had gone to war over Poland —

SENATOR FERGUSON. That is the sad part of it. They went to war over Poland, and there is no Poland today. We went to war over China and China is gone today. . . .

MR. BOHLEN. What I am saying in one sense is that a possible course of action would have been to have stuck by the government in London, that is to say we recognize no other government.

SENATOR FERGUSON. But you don't have to sacrifice all principle.

MR. BOHLEN. I don't think that this is a sacrifice of principle insofar as this agreement goes. I think it was an attempt to do just the opposite. I think it was an attempt to produce a Polish Government in national unity.

SENATOR FERGUSON. Isn't it true at Yalta, so far as Poland is concerned, so far as international law is concerned, that the sovereign rights of an allied country were violated, according to what we envisaged when we signed the Atlantic Charter? Isn't that true?

MR. BOHLEN. I don't quite see —

SENATOR FERGUSON. We divided Poland without Poland being present. We broke off recognition of the London government.

We, Great Britain, and France recognized the present Polish Government, which is nothing more or less than a satellite of the Soviet Union, and wasn't that all in violation of the principles of the Atlantic Charter?

MR. BOHLEN. I just don't read the Atlantic Charter to indicate there should be no territorial adjustments of any kind, and I would like to call your attention to the fact that this arrangement specifically says:

... expresses the view of three heads of the governments consider the eastern frontier of Poland should follow the Curzon line. They recognize that Poland must receive substantial accessions of territory in the north and west.

That is an expression of view. It is perfectly possible to quarrel with the expression of view, but the map of Poland is not as a result thereof, and I will give you an illustration to show you how little, unfortunately, any of these things mattered in Eastern Europe. Neither the United States Government nor the British Government nor the French Government were ever consulted about a certain part of Czechoslovakia. The Czech Government ceded that part to the Soviet Union, and it is now just as much a part of the Soviet Union as anything else.

SENATOR FERGUSON. We didn't consent to that. We, through a lack of interest, haven't recognized the governments in the Baltic States, but they are gone.

MR. BOHLEN. It seems to me almost everything you can think of has been tried in relation to the areas which the Russians ended the war in control of, and I would say that there would be a really serious charge against any of these agreements if they handed over to Russia something that she did not have.

I look upon them as exactly the opposite. You were faced with the fact and not a theory, and what you were attempting to do through diplomatic instruments was to try and express what you hoped to see in those countries through the medium of these instrumentalities which have been violated.

SENATOR FERGUSON. And we also entered into them.

MR. BOHLEN. Well, sir, if the wording of these agreements in places here reflect in your opinion things that were improper, I think your criticism is correct.

SENATOR FERGUSON. I think it is as far as the Curzon line is concerned.

MR. BOHLEN. The Curzon line I think is a legitimate case. President Roosevelt told Mikolajczyk our position was that there should be no territorial settlements until the peace treaty. I think what began to happen, and it was particularly true in the British mind, was that by the time you came to the peace settlement the game might be totally up. There wouldn't have been any need to settle. . . .

SENATOR FERGUSON. You put men in the State Department. You put them there on the assumption that as advisers to the

President they will use judgment. We all talk about hindsight. Good judgment doesn't require you to use hindsight.

MR. BOHLEN. This supposition that this particular treaty (1945 U.S.S.R. China Treaty) was instrumental in bringing about the downfall of Chiang Kai-shek I do not think is the case.

Was it suggested that it would have been preferable to have had no treaty between the Soviet Union and China, to have left that a wide-open breach, or is it meant that the treaty could have been better than it is? Everything could be better, Senator, but it seems to me that every country must learn through its own mistakes, and I think the first task is to identify those mistakes correctly.

SENATOR FERGUSON. I think the saddest thing of all in relation to history is that we don't learn from history.

MR. BOHLEN. One of the things I have felt is these Yalta agreements obviously show imperfections, and I can assure you many of them, the one on Poland was not a happy agreement for anybody connected with it. The President spoke on that point I believe before Congress after Yalta. He was very unhappy about it.

SENATOR FERGUSON. But we agreed to it.

MR. BOHLEN. We felt it was the best we could do. The alternative of doing nothing was worse. That was the judgment.

I would like to say this: A great deal of the moral position of the United States in the leadership accepted by the free world is due to the fact that an honest attempt was made to see if any form of arrangement with the Soviet Union could be arrived at that would have any value for the future of the world. Without that attempt, it would seem to me you would have a much more divided opinion throughout the free world as to who was to blame.

People would say, "How do you know? You didn't try it." These things are all very complicated. History will deal with it and I would not undertake to say that these agreements couldn't have been done better, but I do know this much: that if there had been no Yalta Conference, I sincerely doubt very much if the map of the world would look very different.

I do not think Yalta was the cause. I think Yalta was more a result of certain matters affecting the conduct of the war, certain realities that existed in the world which cannot be changed by wishing they were not there.

SENATOR FERGUSON. But it places our government in the position of having consented to this map of the world.

MR. BOHLEN. No, sir; I don't think so. I don't think that is true. If you wish to say the Iron Curtain stopped at the Curzon line, I think we would all be very, very much happier. The Iron Curtain is on the Elbe, which had nothing whatsoever to do with Yalta. . . .

THE CHAIRMAN. Looking at it from circumstances as they exist today, what would you say?

MR. BOHLEN. That is very hard today. As I testified before, I think from a technical point of view there could always have been improvements in the texts of these agreements, but given the circumstances, I have never been able to see afterward that you could have done much more that would have been of benefit to Poland or the Polish people.

I will testify to my deep conviction that what was animating President Roosevelt and Prime Minister Churchill was a desire to do the very best that they could for Poland.

THE CHAIRMAN. I would like to get this matter plainly before us. As I understand it, your position is that in spite of the promises made in the Atlantic Charter, conditions at that time as they appeared to Roosevelt and the others were such that this was the best arrangement that could be made. Is that correct?

MR. BOHLEN. That is my opinion, sir. . . .

# Suggestions for Additional Reading

Additional primary source material on the Yalta Conference can be found in all of the first-hand accounts from which the excerpts on the preceding pages were taken. For complete coverage, these should be read in their entirety. Another participant who has recorded his recollections is Admiral William D. Leahy in *I Was There* (New York 1948). Some of these memoirs contain valuable material on the events before and after Yalta, especially those of Byrnes, Churchill, and Sherwood.

As there is no published bibliography on the Yalta controversy, the student will have to search for himself in the standard reference guides to the press, periodicals, and government publications. With respect to the many specific problems raised in the course of the debate, what follows is of course highly selective and incomplete.

Favorable discussions of Yalta are to be found in: Wickham Steed, "Fulfillment," *Contemporary Review*, 167 (March 1945) 129–134; Henry Steele Commager, "Was Yalta a Calamity? A Debate," *New York Times Magazine*, August 3, 1952; Raymond Gram Swing, "What Really Happened at Yalta," *New York Times Magazine*, February 20, 1949; McGeorge Bundy, "The Test of Yalta," *Foreign Affairs*, 27 (July 1949) 618–629; Rudolph A. Winnacker, "Yalta, Another Munich?" *Virginia Quarterly Review*, 24 (October 1948) 521–537. For a defense of the Far Eastern agreements as well as some comments on other phases of the conference, see Sumner Welles, *Seven Decisions That Shaped History* (New York 1951), Chs. 5–7.

Considerations of space have precluded the use of the earliest condemnations of Yalta, but their substance is included in those later selections which have been used. Some of the most vigorous of these, focusing naturally on the Polish Agreement, are: Eugene Lyons, "Appeasement in Yalta," *American Mercury*, 60 (April 1945) 461–468; Oswald Garrison Villard, "Poland, A Moral Issue," *Christian Century*, 62 (March 14, 1945) 334–336; Representative Alvin E. O'Konski, speech in the *Congressional Record*, Volume 91, 79th Congress, 1st Session, 1069–1072. Two other sharp criticisms of the settlements affecting Poland, written against a background of Polish problems, are: Arthur Bliss Lane, *I Saw Poland Betrayed* (New York 1948), and Jan Ciechanowski, *Defeat in Victory* (New York 1947). Adverse comments on the secret agreements regarding the U. N. are to be found in *The Private Papers of Senator Vandenberg*, edited by Arthur H. Vandenberg, Jr. (Boston 1952).

For a better grasp of William Henry Chamberlin's "revisionism," the entire book which is excerpted here should be read, as well as a later one, *Beyond Containment* (Chicago 1953), especially Ch. 2. Likewise, Chester Wilmot's analysis is more completely developed in the remainder of his book. A similar view to that of Wilmot is developed in Hanson Baldwin, *Great Mistakes of the War* (New York 1949), and by the same writer in "Churchill Was Right," *Atlantic*, 194 (July 1954) 23–32.

The most hotly debated aspect of Yalta is that involving China. Many have regarded Yalta as a key mistake in bringing on postwar difficulties in this area. Often, there has been a desire to fix and apportion responsibility for these difficulties among certain individuals both in and out of public life. This desire has led to recrimination and partisanship, and has kept Yalta in the forefront of controversy over our Far Eastern policy. Three of the sharpest attacks on both the policy and the personal level are: John T. Flynn, *While You Slept: Our Tragedy in Asia and Who Made It* (New York 1951); Senator Joseph McCarthy, *America's Retreat from Victory: The Story of George Catlett Marshall* (New York 1952); Freda Utley, *The China Story* (Chicago 1951). Two other criticisms of our Far Eastern policy and of Yalta are: William C. Bullitt, "Report to the American People on China," *Life*, October 13, 1947, and "Report of Certain Members of the Joint Armed Services and Foreign Relations Committee of the U. S. Senate," *Hearings on the Military Situation in the Far East*, 82nd Congress, 1st Session, 1951, pp. 3567–3605. The official version of our China policy is found in the U. S. State Department White Paper, *U. S. Relations with China* (Washington 1949). More sympathetic with official policy than those authors cited above, yet not uncritical, are: Herbert Feis, *The China Tangle: The American Effort in China from Pearl Harbor to the Marshall Mission* (Princeton 1953), and Kenneth S. La Tourette, *The American Record in the Far East, 1945–1952* (New York 1952).

On the matter of American Intelligence at the time of Yalta and the condition of Japan at the time, see (in addition to those works of his cited in the readings) Admiral Ellis M. Zacharias, *Behind Closed Doors* (New York 1950). There was much testimony on this subject at the MacArthur Inquiry (cited above). See, for instance, pp. 2914–2917, 3055–3056,

3112–3113, 3119–3120, 3591. For George Marshall's statement, see pp. 561–564. On MacArthur's position in 1945, see Walter Millis (ed.), *The Forrestal Diaries* (New York 1951), p. 31.

Students who wish to locate arguments and fragments of arguments in government publications might begin with the following periods during which the Yalta controversy was especially prominent: (1) February to April of 1945, the period of immediate Congressional reaction and official explanation. (2) May, 1951, the time of the great debate on American foreign policy, following the dismissal of Gen. Douglas MacArthur. (3) February–March, 1953, the period during which the new Republican administration proposed a repudiation of the Yalta agreements. For the official text of this repudiation, see U. S. State Department Bulletin, 28 (March 2, 1953) 353. (4) The spring of 1954, during which time Senator John Bricker led the attempt to amend the U. S. Constitution by limiting the treaty-making powers of the President.

Some of the following books, many with bibliographies, may be helpful in placing Yalta in broader perspective. On international politics and diplomacy, Hans J. Morgenthau, *Politics among Nations* (New York 1954). On the United Nations, a start can be made in Daniel S. Cheever and H. Field Haviland, *Organizing for Peace* (Boston 1954).

On Soviet foreign policy, Max Beloff, *The Foreign Policy of Russia, 1929–1941*, 2 Vols. (New York 1948–49); Harriet L. Moore, *Soviet Far Eastern Policy, 1931–1945* (Princeton 1945); Max Beloff, *Soviet Policy and the Far East, 1944–1951;* James T. Shotwell and Max Laserson, *Poland and Russia, 1919–1945* (New York 1945). A personal memoir on Poland is Stanislaw Mikolajzyk, *The Rape of Poland* (New York 1948).

On U. S. foreign policy, two annual publications present the best description of recent American policy and the problems involved. They are: *The United States in World Affairs*, put out by The Council on Foreign Relations (New York), and *Problems in U. S. Foreign Policy*, put out by the Brookings Institute (Washington). For diplomatic history, see Thomas A. Bailey, *A Diplomatic History of the American People* (New York 1950), and Samuel F. Bemis, *A Diplomatic History of the United States* (New York 1950). Also, see A. Whitney Griswold, *The Far Eastern Policy of the United States* (New York 1938).

On U. S. Russian relations, John R. Deane, *The Strange Alliance: The Story of Our Efforts at Wartime Cooperation with the Russians* (New York 1947); Vera M. Dean, *The United States and Russia* (Cambridge 1947); Thomas A. Bailey, *America Faces Russia* (New York 1950); Raymond Dennet and Joseph E. Johnson (ed.), *Negotiating with the Russians* (Boston 1951).

Two of the best interpretive studies of our strength and weaknesses in foreign relations are George F. Kennan, *Ameri-can Diplomacy, 1900–1950* (Chicago 1951) and Dexter Perkins, *The American Approach to Foreign Policy* (Cambridge 1952). In this vein, see also Gabriel Almond, *The American People and Foreign Policy* (New York 1950).

On the institutional and political problems involved, Elmer Plischke, *The Conduct of American Diplomacy* (New York 1950); Edward S. Corwin, *The President, Office and Powers* (New York 1948); Harold Laski, "The American President and Foreign Relations," in *The Presidency in Transition*, edited by Robert S. Rankin (Gainesville 1949), pp. 171–205; Robert A. Dahl, *Congress and Foreign Policy* (New Haven 1949); William Y. Elliott (Chairman), *United States Foreign Policy, Its Organization and Control* (New York 1952).

In addition to those already cited or used in the preceding pages, two of the best personal memoirs for filling in the study of foreign policy in this period are Cordell Hull, *The Memoirs of Cordell Hull* (New York 1948) and Walter Bedell Smith, *My Three Years in Moscow* (Philadelphia 1950).